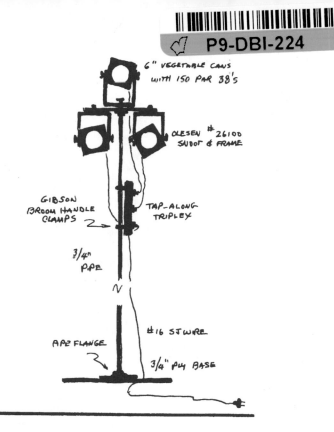

STAGE LIGHTING

IN THE boondocks

A layman's handbook of down-to-earth
methods of lighting theatricals
with limited resources

BY JAMES HULL MILLER

MERIWETHER PUBLISHING LTD.
Colorado Springs, Colorado

Meriwether Publishing Ltd., Publisher
P.O. Box 7710
Colorado Springs, CO 80933

Typesetting: Sharon E. Garlock
Cover design: Gerald Moscato
Illustrations: James Hull Miller

Library of Congress Cataloging-in-Publication Data

Miller, James Hull.
        Stage lighting in the boondocks : a layman's handbook of down-to-earth methods of lighting theatricals with limited resources / by James Hull Miller. -- 4th ed..
        p. c.m.
        ISBN 1-56608-017-7
        1. Stage lighting. 2. Amateur theater--Production and direction.
    I. Title.
    PN2091.E4M5   1995
    792'.025--dc20

                                                                95-22366
                                                                CIP

Contents

FOREWORD

The fact that you have picked up this book and are reading it indicates that you are probably facing some sort of crisis in lighting a play. You feel beleaguered and are seeking help. Now there are four entirely different situations in which you may find yourself, and as you read through this book it is important to identify the situation you are in.

1.

You have been asked to light a play which is being done in a church or an assembly hall of some sort, possibly with a small concert platform. You will have to use whatever current supply exists and you will be bringing your own equipment. Perhaps you have made some yourself.

2.

You have been asked to light a more ambitious project such as a musical comedy or an opera to be staged in some school auditorium that is woefully underequipped. For this operation you will probably rent or purchase some sort of dimmer board for which you will need an electrical connection. You will also need lots of electrical cable for the lights you bring. When you depart, all this equipment will go with you. This is somewhat akin to a professional road show playing in a rented commercial theatre although not of the same scale. Aside from the electrical connection made by a licensed contractor, you are dealing with items "off the shelf," that is, stock units that are easily purchased.

3.

You are involved with remodeling an old building such as a chapel or meeting hall. In this case, you will be making a permanent installation and the wiring must conform to local electrical codes, and the circuits for the stage lighting will have to terminate in a cross-connecting panel leading to the dimmers. For this project you will need help, either assistance from equipment manufacturers or from independent theatre consultation.

You find yourself in the planning of a future project that will be built from scratch. For this you will definitely need independent theatre consultation for you are now involved with owners, architects and engineers, not to mention the staff, both present and future! In other words, a lot of money is going to be spent and there must be adequate planning. There will also be a considerable current supply to be reckoned with. You are no longer in the boondocks.

For the first three situations you should acquire the trade directories which list manufacturers and suppliers of theatrical products geographically. Currently these are:

Lighting Dimensions Buyers' Guide

Lighting Dimensions Directory

**Theatre Crafts Directory of
Manufacturers, Suppliers & Consultants**

All are available from:
Theatre Crafts
135 Fifth Avenue
New York, NY 10010-7193

For all situations I suggest membership in the **U.S. Institute for Theatre Technology, Inc., 10 West 19th St., Suite 5A, New York, NY 10010-4206**. The Institute holds an annual conference and an industry-wide trade show, usually in the spring.

INTRODUCTION

I "fell" into theatre quite by accident in 1934 when, as a freshman at Princeton, I needed to earn some money to "make ends meet," it being the aftermath of Black Friday and the Great Depression. The job I had involved the Student Express — we moved anything and everything we could get our hands on. So early one rainy autumn morning I found myself by a railroad siding, unloading sets for **Ethan Frome**, a Broadway show on tour. That was the beginning of it and I have been backstage ever since. In the early years I built just about anything that came along, but in later years I specialized in low-cost scenery and lighting systems that would be useful in any sort of space where a performance might take place. I did so because I did not observe many others doing much about such situations — and I felt I had some ideas that would be useful.

This book deals with down-to-earth methods of lighting theatricals for live audiences. It is written for the beginner who has limited resources and little experience. The book is in two parts: the first gives some basic solutions for a number of specific spaces and programs; the second contains information on a series of related subjects such as spotlight types, dimmers, lamps, filters, connectors, etc. and includes a section on homemade equipment.

The main purpose of this book is to "bring light to bear" primarily upon the actor and the scenery and props in a reasonable and inexpensive manner. The important thing to realize, though, is that all contemporary lighting effects, to some degree, are within reach of the amateur's pocketbook, with the payoff through artful use rather than by means of sophisticated equipment.

Thus, **Stage Lighting in the Boondocks** *is addressed to the technician whose "back is to the wall," so to speak, and whose resources are largely matters of his own inventive spirit — helped, I hope, by the contents of this book.*

James H. Miller

PART I
Lighting Specific Places and Programs

CHAPTER 1

The Art of Stage Lighting

We watch the late afternoon sun streaking in below a large cloud mass after a spring shower. We see the delicate shadows of bare trees upon aleaf-strewn lawn in Indian summer, or the thin gold dusk of a winter afternoon. And we exclaim, "The lighting is so dramatic." And rightly so, for dramatic illumination awakens our sensibilities. It "puts things in a fresh light," to use a figurative phrase quite literally.

There is a great deal of mystique surrounding stage lighting: slang terms for specialized equipment, the "sacredness" of cur sheets, etc. But good lighting really amounts to little more than getting some illumination onto a particular scene from the best possible angles and then being able to control the intensities of the various light sources. One reason that the lighting for Broadway shows is constantly acclaimed is that designers assemble rental equipment from scratch for each production, whereas the dullness of lighting in most "institutional" theatres can be attributed to the fact that spotlights are usually purchased along with the building — thus they tend to remain where they are first installed...and infrequently relocated thereafter. Furthermore, with modern "memory" control boards there is also the temptation not to refocus the lighting units once their positions have been recorded.

There are four reasons for specialized lighting in the theatre. The first is *visibility*, and so important is this that I like to use a frontal fill or wash more or less aligned with the audience axis. The second reason is *dramatic interest*, achieved through variously placed lights. Third, lighting must *focus* attention. This is why so many dimmers are used in the theatre, in order that areas of interest can be highlighted at will. (In motion pictures and television this is done by changing the camerfa position.) And fourth, lighting creates the *mood* of a scene. We should be able to distinguish night from day, sunny from cloudy days, and eerie from ordinary scenes.

One might begin with a little knowledge about the nature of

light itself. Categorically, there are two principal types of light: diffuse and specular. These types may be distinguished by the nature of their shadows. Generally speaking, the wider the light source the less defined the shadow will be. Most light around us is a combination of these two types. When it is not we are immediately aware of the lack of balance. Examples are photographs taken on the surface of the moon where an absence of atmosphere makes the sun a totally specular source; and contrariwise, days on earth when a heavy cloud cover causes objects to lose definition. Other examples are foggy days or automobile headlights in the country on a moonless night. In the theatre a scoop is a diffuse source of light; a spotlight, a specular one.

Diagrammed below is a simple exercise in the art of lighting. Mount the spotlights on stands at the heights indicated. Connect each light to a separate dimmer and place the controllers in the audience position. Experiment with various intensities until the scene is lit to your satisfaction. Then note the various dimmer readings. By this exercise you will understand that the purpose of the frontal or fill light is for visibility and that the more sharply angled lights create the sculptural form and the dramatic interest. You will also note that the frontal light will have the lowest reading while the backlighting may have the highest.

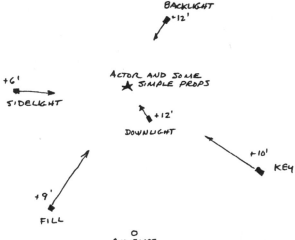

4

This exercise speaks for itself in that it points up the tremendous flexibility of stage lighting especially where there is the freedom to position the lighting sources. This is the first lesson. The second lesson is the ability to control the brilliance of each lighting source. Third, and in my opinion the least important, are the types of lights.

It is obvious that one can't apply this particular formula for lighting to every scene in the threatre. Sometimes scenery will be in the way as with box sets. Some mounting postions are not always available. Special effects may dictate novel approaches. And the degree of audience surround may complicate things, as in arena staging. However, these five positions are fundamental ones and make good sense for a starter.

In these times almost everyone who is involved with stage lighting is aware to some degree of lighting arrangements for photograp;hy and television and the considerable differences from those for the theatre. Playing to live audiences involves the human eye, that incredible seeing machine which tolerates a range of brightness contrast from 1000:1. Once, during a power failure in a small arena theatre, I saw a memorable performance of Ibsen's *Ghosts* by light from a single candelabra. On the other hand tolerances for film and television are far less: film being 100:1, television 40:1. Of these facts a theatre technician should be aware, for he will be shopping in the same market places that are largely dominated by these entertainment industries. Their needs and his needs may vary greatly.

On a visit to the TV studio you will notice how large and bulky the diffuse sources are. One problem in theatre lighting is where to locate these diffuse sources so that they are visually unobstusive and unwanted "spill" minimized with a live audience present. For this reason much theatrical lighting falls somewhere between what would be ideal and what is possible. In the previous examples "fill" was accomplished by Fresnel spotlights whereas in a studio some sort of "softlight" would have been used such as the bouncing of light off large white matte surfaces or passing light through large diffuse filters.

Other differences in studio lighting have to do with the "whiteness" of light, a closer balance between bright and dim areas, and a higher intensity of light than we normally need in the theatre. These are technical matters which have to do with the sensitivity of film emulsion and the receptivity of television cameras. So long as the theatrical technician is lighting for a *live* audience he may disregard these differences (though he cannot escape them entirely).

Below, a simple scene, a small pavilion at dusk, is sketched out and diagrammed. Let's see how the lighting plot described above might be applied to such a scene. But first it will be necessary to identify further two primary sources of illumination mentioned thus far, the Fresnel and ellipsoidal spotlights. The Fresnel uses a type of lens which produces an inherently

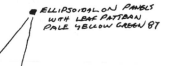

TRANSLUCENT PANELS

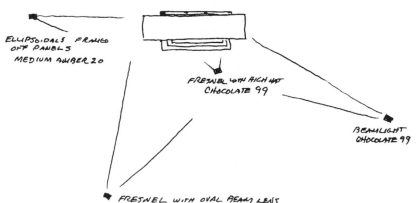

ELLIPSOIDAL ON PANELS
WITH LEAF PATTERN
PALE YELLOW GREEN 87

ROSCOLUX COLORS

ELLIPSOIDALS FRAMED
OFF PANELS
MEDIUM AMBER 20

FRESNEL WITH RICH HOT
CHOCOLATE 99

BEAMLIGHT
CHOCOLATE 99

FRESNEL WITH OVAL BEAM LENS
PALE YELLOW 07

soft-edged field of light. Its spread can be varied, but it cannot be precisely matted. The ellipsoidal employs a type of lens system which makes possible the precise shaping of the light beam through internal matting shutters. The term Fresnel refers to the inventor of this particular lens design. The term ellipsoidal refers to a carefully designed lamp reflector which maximizes the candle power of a lamp filament in conjunction with an objective lens system. The ellipsoidal is often called a Leko, an acronym after the founders of a lighting company which popularized it. The two types are not interchangeable in performance value as will be explain in a later section.

The choice of an ellipsoidal spotlight for the backlight is a natural one since the beam can be precisely matted by means of the inbuilt shutters, thus the translucent panels can be lit without spill elsewhere. Further, any number of foliage patterns may be inserted into a pattern slot that can be specified. An ellipsoidal spotlight is also chosen for the sidelighting to prevent light from splashing onto the translucent panels. If there is a considerable amount of downstage movement several spotlights may be necessary, possibly some Fresnels with high hats for the farther downstage areas.

A Fresnel spotlight with a high hat is selected for the sharply angled downlight because of soft-edged field is more desirable since an actor may walk in and ut of the shaft. This spotlight may have to be moved farther upstage so that it is directly over the platform and steps to avoid splashing onto the translucent panels. In this latter position it can be aimed slightly downstage and become a backlight of sorts. The frontal fill *must* be soft-edged, and a Fresnel is called for. The old Kliegl oval beam Fresnel lens would do the trick nicely since it spreads the field in a 3/2 proportion and an actor could be coverfed without including a great amount of forestage or roof. However, this lens has gone off the market and an ellipsoidal spotlight with a Rosco 104 tough Silk diffusion filter will do much the same thing.

The key or modeling light from the forward side should also have a soft edge since some light is bound to fall upon the translucent panels as well. A beamlight has been chosen to soften any shadows. A beamlight has not been mentioned thus far. It is a type of narrow beam floodlight and is described in the section on lighting fixture design.

In terms of intensity, the backlight and sharply angled downlight will be quite brilliant. The sidelight need not be quite as bright, nor the key light. But the fill should be turned down as low as possible consistent with visibility since it will be lighting the translucent panels as well. Rosculux Pale Yellow 07 is selected because it is one of the few colors that can take a considerable amount of dimming without an appreciable change of color hue. (When lamps are dimmed they lose some of their "whiteness" with consequent adverse effects on many color filters. Along with Roscolux Pale Yellow 07, Chocolate 99 and Daylight Blue 65 are good "neutrals" that can also take considerable dimming.)

Two additional scenes present variations of these fundamental lighting positions. The first is from *Hamlet III, 3,* the familiar chapel scene:

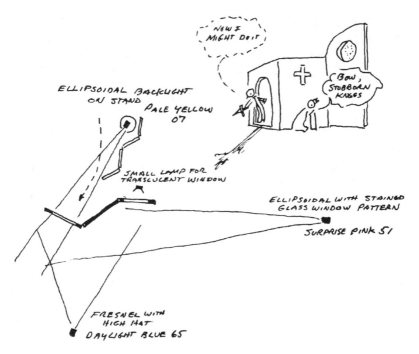

The second is a simple interior by candlelight, with moonlight outside.

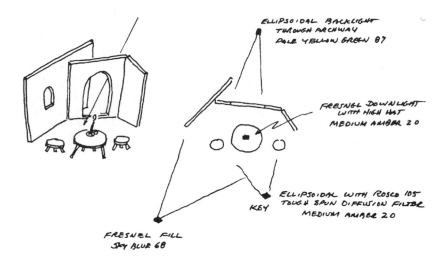

ELLIPSOIDAL BACKLIGHT
THROUGH ARCHWAY
PALE YELLOW GREEN 87

FRESNEL DOWNLIGHT
WITH HIGH HAT
MEDIUM AMBER 20

ELLIPSOIDAL WITH ROSCO 105
TOUGH SPUN DIFFUSION FILTER
MEDIUM AMBER 20

KEY

FRESNEL FILL
SKY BLUE 68

CHAPTER 2

Lighting the High School Auditorium

Usually the school auditorium is a concert hall built in the image of a theatre — a combination which compromises the best features of each while compounding the worst! From a theatrical viewpoint, the proscenium is overly wide at the expense of the wings. There is some rigging, but no fly loft. The stage depth is limited, but the apron is considerable. From a concert viewpoint, the overhead teasers and the ubiquitous stage drapes make the poorest of sound reflectors — besides, these are, with the exception of the main curtain, inflexibly hung by dead-chaining them to the structure overhead. As for illumination, the majority of stage lighting is installed well upstage and boxed in by these same teasers; what little frontal lighting exists comes from relatively inaccessible ceiling coves. And to avoid a steeply pitched auditorium seating, the stage is abnormally high. In this way an orchestra pit can be avoided.

Despite this functional chaos, auditoriums continue to be built and equipped in the same way over and over again perhaps because such a design makes about as much sense as any other for such a potpourri of programming. The cheerleaders can swing on their ropes. Paper backdrops and paper-covered flats can be painted by just about anyone, and are endlessly recycled. To the public at large, curtains symbolize theatre, and of such curtains there are a goodly number even if most of them are made of that vinyl-coated imitation fabric so stiff that they move aside rather than give when nudged.

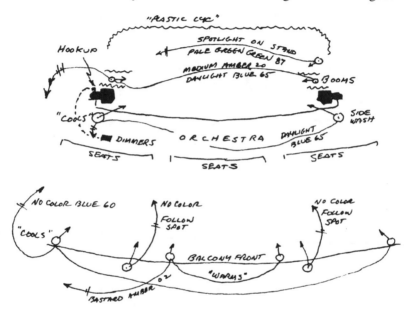

For many years I helped with the presentation of symphony operas on just such a stage. In many respects I did a better job with these operas than later on when the symphony was ensconced in a new civic theatre.

The diagram shows a 50'-wide stage 4' above the auditorium floor. There is a 7' apron and 15' of space upstage of the curtain line. The balcony front is 35' from the apron.

Four 1000-watt 8" Fresnel spotlights with Kliegl 3/2 Oval Beam lenses were secured to the balcony front and paired as shown to cover the entire stage with both "warm" and "cool" color washes. (This type of lens is no longer available and to obtain the same lateral coverage today, a third spotlight would have to be added to

12

each pair.) In addition, there were two 1000-watt 8" ellipsoidal spotlights with iris and shutter controls and with wooden handles on short stands. These spotlights had beam spreads of about 18°. On the auditorium floor to each side of the apron were 12' light stands with a 1000-watt 8" Fresnel spotlight on each. These spotlights created a cross wash of soft-edged illumination. Upstage of the proscenium were sidelighting spotlights (commonly called "booms") consisting of two 500-watt wide-beam ellipsoidal spotlights to each side. Further upstage was a single 500-watt 6" Fresnel spotlight on an 8' stand, usually with a Pale Yellow Green gel. I regarded this particular location and fixture as my "signature" and used this spotlight to advantage on every opera I lit.

The dimmers were of the autotransformer type with two packages of three 2000-watt Powerstats each plus several 1000-watt dimmers in homemade cases. (Today I would use two SCR six-channel 2400-watt packs remotely located, with controllers in the same orchestra position.) The hookup was through two 50-amp range plug receptacles adjacent to the backstage control board for the school's lighting system which, with the exception of house lighting, was not used for the operas. In addition, there were 14 small 10" scoops with 200-watt PS IF lamps for use behind ground rows and set piece windows, and for general backing illumination.

Our lighting technique was an incredibly simple one. All spotlights with the exception of the two 8" ellipsoidals in the balcony were used for washes. The two balcony ellipsoidals were used for all "specials." The operators could tilt and pan them, and iris them in the manner of follow spots — but they were not to be used "in motion," rather, in *momentarily fixed* positions. The operators were furnished no cue sheets. Instead, with the spotlights irised down, they would watch through the ventilating slots for the lamps to come on dim, a signal for an upcoming cue such as one of those frequent times when the singers stand still for a solo, duet, or small choral ensemble. Then the operators would crack their irises slightly, enabling them to "get on target" while I raised their intensities and reduced those of the wash lights. The operators were instructed never to follow a singer but to close down upon anticipation of a group breaking up as I rebalanced the general illumination. Since I was within view of the operators I would be able to unobtrusively indicate with an index finger situations where the spotlights were to be used separately.

It is obvious that only in opera (with its slow pace and limited stage movement) could such a technique work; and it was a technique that depended upon operators who continually observed the dramatic action, as indeed they should with all good lighting! Needless to say, this technique did not survive a subsequent move to a new civic theatre with its backstage control board and the heavy hands of union electricians on the dimmers. Further, it should be noted that with such "bare bones" equipment as much special lighting as possible was built into the scenery itself: street lamps, lanterns, the glow of shaded windows, etc.

This example of inserting some functional lighting into a poorly equipped school auditorium gets our "foot in the door" of many of the possibilities of stage lighting "in the boondocks." We have come a long way with a minimum of basic lighting units strategically placed and controlled. Where do we go from here? We go in two directions: obviously we need more lighting equipment for most dramatic situations; on the other hand, many of those handed the challenge of lighting "in the boondocks" will have limited experience — for these, some instructions in the art of lighting follow.

CHAPTER 3

Lighting Little Theatres and Civic Theatres

One generally associates the phrase "little theatre" with the predominately amateur community theatre movement dating chiefly from the early 1920s and inspired by the new continental stagecraft and its East Coast prototypes such as the Provincetown Playhouse on Cape Cod and the Theatre Guild in New York. *Theatre Arts Magazine* was the voice of that era, heralding a "grass-roots" movement dubbed the "Tributary Theatre," though the ideas and plays continued to flow the other way.

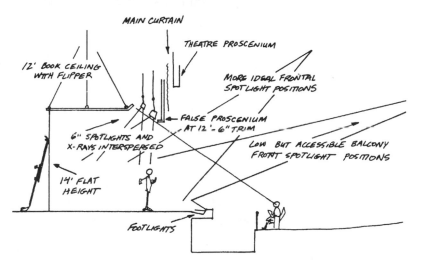

Overall, the "little theatre" movement has been proscenium-oriented, and the prevailing style of scenery has been illusory in nature. Most of the plays of this era called for sets showing domestic interiors and a proscenium frame simplifies this type of setting, the so-called "box" set, that is, a box with one side missing. A partial ceiling piece enforces the literal illusion. The proximity and all-encompassing nature of this kind of scenery presents some difficult lighting challenges, and a specialized system of lighting such spaces evolved which has little to do with the lighting examples presented thus far.

This system was encapsulated in a little book called *A Method of Lighting the Stage*, by Stanley McCandless (1931). Paramount is the idea of dividing the stage into a series of acting zones and then crosslighting each zone from approximately 45° above and to each side with both "warm" and "cool" colors, the motivation for which depended upon some illusory feature of the setting such as sunlight pouring through a window or a fireplace or table lamp, etc. Known as the McCandless System, this technique will be valid as long as there are proscenium stages with box sets. Obviously the system has little application to thrust stages and other types of open stages, and to arena stages, none at all.

Lighting for these highly literal box sets by necessity should combine elements of both diffuse and specular light. The sculptural form of the actor must be maintained by spotlights yet floodlighting must blend the various pools of light, smooth out spill on the set and provide realistic overall illumination. And what is more, all this must be accomplished with little possibility of backlighting, limited sidelighting and with very short throws from proscenium masked positions. Thus, every available inch was utilized, with small spotlights and floods crammed across the proscenium and down its sides.

X-ray compartment type borderlights and baby spots were the order of the day. "X-ray" was a trade name for a type of reflector widely used in store window displays in the 1920s. It provided a highly diffused source of illumination. Units were usually 6' long, with 12"-square compartments. Each unit was wired for three-color circuits. Gel frames were fitted over the compartment openings. One no longer finds these units in catalogs though the term still surfaces on many road show technical requirement sheets. Unfortunately, no true substitute exists, the present 6" compartment type borderlights with internal reflector lamps leaving much to be desired in the way of a really soft, diffuse illumination.

"Baby spots" were small spotlights with 4½" diameter planoconvex lenses, ideal for cramming into small spaces though they were neither very bright nor efficient. But while the light beam was basically specular there are ways to diffuse the sharp edges by cutting the centers from frost gels or making photographer's sawtoothed mats. Eventually the baby spot was replaced by the more efficient Fresnel lens spotlight.

Footlights were also useful, and the more diffuse the illumination the better. The best were made up of banks of the smallest possible compartments into which small A-type lamps were inserted base first. Color frames with tinted filters were used. With the advent of the thrust stage and the partial audience surround most good footlights have all but disappeared.

Box sets were room sets and rooms have a lot of doors. Behind these doors backing flats were placed, representing other rooms or hallways. A method of lighting these backings was needed, and in the limited space the backing striplight was devised. They were usually made of metal and painted aluminum or white gloss inside. No provision was made for color filters. If color was desired, dipped lamps were used. A hook was provided for hanging over a toggle of an adjacent flat. Since this particular unit was made of wood, 40 watts is the largest lamp that should be used. Once standard equipment, these units have disappeared from the marketplace.

One big problem with little theatre box set lighting lies in the downstage area where the actors move out from under a veritable bath of fuzzy light and very short-throw cross-spotting into lighting that comes from sources mounted in the auditorium.

In most older theatres the opportunity for frontlighting was limited by mounting positions that were too low, such as the balcony front and too far to the side, such as the proscenium boxes. It was also difficult to keep light from spilling onto the proscenium, thus distracting from a literal illusion. The first problem was eventually solved by building theatres with better auditorium mounting facilities. The second problem has been partially solved by the introduction of a newer type of spotlight, the ellipsoidal reflector, with an objective lens system and adjustable shutters which permit precise matting. But this solution brought its own problem: the mixture of hard-edged specular light with the more diffuse illumination within the proscenium frame. The nature of this light beam is inherently hard-edged, contrasting with the softer illumination within the proscenium, thus making the blending of these two forms of light most difficult, if not impossible.

Not shown on the drawing is another source of diffuse light: narrow open trough striplights which can be attached to the rear of sets adjacent to doorways, etc. to illuminate approaching actors as well as backing flats suggesting hallways, etc. Though no longer listed in catalogs, these are easily made. Instructions will be found in the Homemade Equipment chapter in Part II.

Outdoor settings for little theatres present other challenges chiefly because of the difficulty of hanging and lighting sky drops. Many little theatres do not have adequate stage lofts and thus have numerous overhead masking teasers which get in the way of the even floodlighting of backdrops. And because of the "illusion of reality" which most proscenium stages create, it goes without saying that no spill from spotlights and such should ever fall on a sky piece, a requirement that can be met only by having enough distance between the acting area and the sky piece, distance often hard to come by in most small community theatres.

On the other hand, old-fashioned "wing-and-border" sets are easily lit on small proscenium stages, for there are ample mounting positions for sidelighting and for overhead borderlight strips. Woodland scenes, melodrama settings on roll drops and even "painted" buildings for operettas are naturals for these compact stages.

Lighting the Civic Theatre

From time to time groups from the boondocks, or even from the suburbs of "the Big Scene" find themselves on those large civic center stages. These stages are designed for a wide range of activities, but to make room for commercial road shows they usually have minimal stage furnishings such as a straight sky drop, several legs and border cloths, a main curtain, perhaps an additional traveler curtain and, invariably, several runs of nearly continuous borderlight strips with R-lamps and glass roundels, and a few 1000-watt 8" Fresnel spotlights interspersed. Out in the auditorium ceiling cove are some ellipsoidal spotlights — usually insufficient both in num-

18

bers and brilliance for action down front. Often there are footlights of the disappearing type whose existence has long been forgotten.

It must be realized that any permanent lighting equipment over the stage has been kept minimal chiefly so that the stage loft is as free as possible for the hanging of road shows which not only bring their own drops and scenery but usually all of their own lighting equipment as well. Thus the civic theatre may be grossly under-equipped for local groups without these resources. And steps must be taken to provide additional equipment, either by rental if for a one-shot deal, or by some combination of rental and gradual purchase if the civic theatre usage is a continuing one.

First check to see how many circuits have been routed to floor pockets. On the average there will be about a dozen 20-amp circuits. Also check on the type of connector used. Then plan to do three things: add spotlights in the auditorium ceiling cove, provide stands and spotlights for sidelighting, and add a row of spotlights on an empty batten that is located well downstage.

The additional auditorium ceiling cove spotlights should be of the ellipsoidal type. Measure both the width of the stage and the distance from the cove to the stage, then consult the performance specifications on spotlight data sheets. It has been my experience that 12 1000-watt 8" spots with field angles of around 15° will fix most any situation. Cables will probably have to run back along the access catwalk and down to floor pockets on the stage.

Equally important is adequate sidelighting. Such equipment is rarely included in the original installation on the grounds that it is "floating" equipment and therefore liable to be stolen. Sidelighting is best accomplished with a combination of 500-watt 6" Fresnel and ellipsoidal spotlights mounted on stands and placed in several wing positions on each side of the stage. A homemade stand is shown on page 18, using ¾" plywood, 1¼" pipe and flanges. The little spotlight near the floor is known as a "shin buster" and is especially important for dance programs. Again, the stage floor electrical pockets will provide the power.

Of lesser importance than the preceding, but often very useful, is the addition of a downstage spotlight batten using a spare pipe from the theatre's rigging system. This will enable the placement of spotlights where needed rather than having to depend on the spotlights sandwiched in between the striplights or at the extreme ends of the striplight battens. Cables are tied along this batten and are dropped down to the already overworked floor pockets.

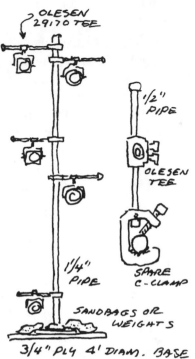

Once the capacity of the floor pockets has been exhausted, attempt to utilize the circuits which are connected to the footlights as these are rarely used anymore. If this fails, you will have to bring in an auxiliary package dimmer board. There will be no problem in connecting this, for if there is one thing that civic theatres have plenty of it is "raw" power for the hooking up of road show boards.

CHAPTER 4

Lighting Arena and Thrust Stages

"Breaking Out" of the Box

During the 1940s arena stages began springing up all over the country. The "prophets" predicted the return to "a theatre for immortals," a "true symbolic theatre," etc. A most scholarly and ecstatic article appeared in the *Educational Theatre Journal [Vol. 4, 1952, p. 11]* entitled "The Cube and the Sphere," wherein proscenium scenes were likened to frozen segments of time and place and free-form scenes to the more ethereal spaces of poetic imagination. However, no such noble changes took place. Romanticism and the painter's art remained firmly entrenched within the proscenium frame while the arena stage made possible the elimination of costly, naturalistic box sets without disturbing the arrangement of the furniture, an accommodation which explains the marked preference for squarish over elliptical or circular playing areas. As for lighting, the Stanley McCandless system gave way to the Kelly Yeaton system, for now one's backlighting is another man's frontlighting, and the delicate subtleties of "warms" and "cools" were lost along with a viable source of diffuse illumination as well.

Simultaneously, another stage form was becoming very fashionable — the open platform stage. This form evolved from dramatic festivals (both ancient and modern) that are heavy on pageantry — with lots of steps and levels and usually some sort of architectural facade as a background. George Kernodle was the archivist with his book *From Art to Theatre,* and Tyrone Guthrie was the high priest, with festival stages in Scotland, Canada and the United States. And again there evolved a lighting system indigenous to this sort of space.

With the exception of the operatic and ballet stages, these new forms shook up the traditionalists a bit but not sufficiently to put a dent into the working loft stagehouse. Instead, the conservatives countered by reshaping the old stage apron into a pseudo-Guthrie form which they named the "thrust stage," an open, tongue-like platform located just ahead of the old proscenium — an uneasy compromise that was the best of all possible worlds to some but the worst to others. For without an inordinate amount of physical rearrangements proscenium sightlines are jeopardized and actors unduly distanced by the presence of the thrust when the dramatic action is not focused upon it. The mechanical engineer to meet this challenge successfully was George Izenour, but his thinly disguised and quite expensive "machines for theatre" lacked the charms of single solution playhouses: the intimacy of the arena, the exquisite mystery of a good proscenium stage, or even the theatricality of the old horseshoe plan with its technically despised but always sought after side boxes.

Lighting Theatre-in-the Round

When one enters the "arena" of lighting a space which is entirely surrounded by audience many of the existing rules change. There is obviously no sidelighting and what is backlighting for some is frontlighting for others. About all that remains the same is downlighting, and this is the only direction from which heavily saturated colors can be used. All else goes to tints for visibility. Contrast must be achieved in subtle ways. The most difficult problem is lighting the playing area and not the audience as well. It is difficult because the audience must be as close as possible to the players without losing a sense of privacy. There is nothing more devastating in arena staging than having too much space. This means that we are talking about a lighting cutoff that is very hard to achieve.

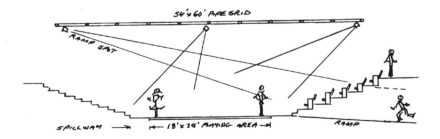

This section is typical of many arena theatres, with the audience seated on the first terrace to minimize "spill." Usually there is some "spill" around the playing area and it is very important that this space be as shallow as possible, and also of a very different appearance; otherwise you are in effect enlarging the playing area and you may lose that vital sense of intimacy. The floor of the playing area should be of a non-splintering hardwood with a proper "spring" for dance, and dark-stained and matte. A beige carpet should be available for comedy. Its soft reflectance will reduce the starkness of overhead lighting, diffuse sources being absent for obvious reasons.

The lighting grid is 18' above the playing area in order to minimize the distraction of having to look at the spotlights. Eighteen feet is about as high as you can go and still use the economical 500-watt spotlights. While egg crate construction would mask many spotlights it is poor acoustically and frustrates maximum flexibility. And difficult though it will be, I recommend ladder service from below rather than catwalks for two reasons: to keep the room volume as compact as possible for acoustics; and to obtain the most flexible spotlight positioning. This will call for pipe instead of Unistrut for the grid since it is easier to secure lights with C-clamps when working from a ladder.

Exclusive of downlighting, you must strike each area from at least three directions with spotlights about 120° apart (the Kelly Yeaton system) or preferably from all four sides. Since a workable area is about 6' square there will be 12 areas in all in the above example, and from 36 to 48 spotlights. Add 12 more for downlights, 3 or 4 more for the entrance ramps and some specials. Half of the spotlights should be standard 6"x9" ellipsoidals, the other half Fresnels with high hat and barn door accessories. The downspots should be wide-beam ellipsoidals with pattern slots. The ramp specials should be narrow-beam ellipsoidals and the remaining specials, narrow-beam beam with iris controls.

To service these spotlights I recommend eight 22'-long plugging strips with eight duplex receptacles each. A patch panel should be located in the control room. Also in the control room should be a 24-channel control system with the standard 2-scene preset, master and independent options, split fader and timed cross-fader. Since this will require electronic dimmers, the dimmer bank should be located in a well-ventilated, acoustically isolated room, for hearing is difficult enough in any arena theatre without additional ambient noise of any sort. Seating area downlights and service lights over the playing area may be operated by wall box transformer dimmers in the control room to avoid having to turn on the electronic dimmer system for such chores as cleaning and early rehearsals.

All this may sound pretty elegant for the "boondocks" — and it is. There is no getting around the fact that having an audience on more sides than one does increase the number of lights. It's one thing to wash down over players with a couple of backlights and quite another to replace those backlights with a complete system suitable for frontal illumination. And you can't get away with a bunch of PARs in tin cans — not if you want a precise cutoff. Thus, lighting is *the* big cost factor in arena theatre.

Lighting the Thrust Stage

In America the arena theatre preceded the thrust stage chiefly because scenic backgrounds were completely eliminated, whereas with the various forms of "open" stages there are backgrounds that have to be dealt with in some fashion — certainly they cannot be ignored. And of all these myriad shapes of open stages, from deep aprons to frank platforms, the one term that has stuck fast has been "thrust," though there is no more logic to this than calling all color filters for stage lights "gels."

In the more extreme forms of a thrust stage it might be assumed that we have, in effect, a 3-sided arena lighting situation, but in actual practice it is not quite the same thing. In the first place, theatricals on the thrust tend to be a little more splashy and roman-tic, and the audience more spectators than voyeurs. In the second place, because of the background, the audience is conscious of a major axis through the playing area and does not expect a uniform distribution of illumination. In the third place, since the audience is only *partially* around the thrust a more diffuse illumination can be used than is found in the pure arena.

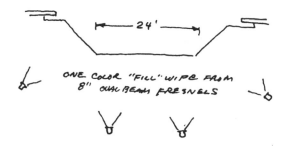

With these conditions in mind, my own approach to lighting on the thrust is the traditional studio technique of soft fill light to the satisfaction of visibility plus more sharply angled spotlights, usually ellipsoidals, for dramatic interpretation. I use pairs of Fresnels across the front of the stage and one or more Fresnels along each side for a single color tint wash. Double the amount for 2-color wash. (If possible, these Fresnels should be fitted with "oval beam" or other spread lenses — otherwise some additional Fresnels may be called for, and some 2-way barn doors required.)

While the audience may not be so steeply canted as in the more intimate arena form, problems do arise where the accommodation of large audiences causes the light grid or ceiling level to be raised to a height above the platform where more powerful spotlights or spotlights of a narrower beam spread may be required. Just a few additional feet can send the price tag soaring both in initial cost and in current consumption. In my experience this breaking point is right at 18' above the stage floor.

For the more historical and romantic sort of plays the stage may be lit entirely with beamlights. These lensless, mirrored-surface parabolic reflector units produce rather narrow shafts of soft-edged light and are quite powerful. Their classic use in North America came with the initial Festival Stage in Ontario, Canada in the early 1950s. There were some 30, in an arc about the stage, at about a 40° approach angle. Each unit was on a separate dimmer. These particular units were from England and called "pageant lanterns." There are definite advantages to this sort of illumination, especially where the stage floor is a highly visible part of the overall background and where the sharp patterns of ellipsoidals are undesirable.

Lecture and Concert Platforms

The lighting for chancel drama and for some thrust stages is similar to that for lecture and concert platforms in that a sophisticated combination of diffuse and selective lighting is necessary, plus a recognition of the fact that overall backgrounds are not always of the producer's choosing but belong to the spaces he is using.

The first problem to attack is entrances. Where possible, all doorways or other openings onto the platform should be masked from view by self-supporting sets of screens (see my book *Self-Supporting Scenery*). The next precaution is to prevent any spill from hard-edged spotlights upon the architectural surfaces surrounding the platform. Where dramatic illumination does wash up onto the walls, use Fresnels, or beamlights, or ellipsoidal spotlights with diffusion filters. The use of scoops is precluded because of their bulk. The final problem involves the mounting of the equipment. My "rule of thumb" is to position the equipment in those locations most advantageous for the "art of lighting" regardless of the methods of mounting. I strongly advocate even the use of spotlight stands in full view if necessary, so long as these stands do not interfere directly with the audience's view of the actor. This is not the place for "cosmetic" dressing. If the show is good, the presence of a forest of stands in quickly forgotten. See the chapter Homemade Equipment in Part II for the design of some stands which do not look unwieldy in space.

26

CHAPTER 5

Lighting Chancel Drama

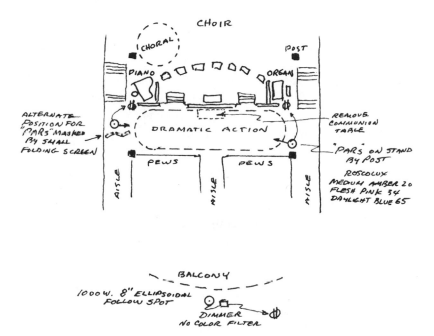

My own approach to lighting in the church sanctuary is to use all of the *existing* illumination that is on the dim side, *then highlight* the performance area with the least amount of theatrical equipment that will get the job done. By adding only scenery that is truly free-standing, the church will retain its architectural identity and serve as the overall background; the pew area will have sufficient illumination for the scanning of hymns; and the minimal equipment, discreetly placed, will not attract undue attention.

You will find that this approach wins approval with church elders, for you must realize that a church is a symbol of faith, and any dilution or alteration of its identity may appear even sacrilegious to some. Another good way of not "rocking the boat" is to

27

bring only that amount of equipment which can be connected to existing electrical outlets of the parallel blade type. There may be more separately fused branch circuits than you would suspect. This means using individual dimmers rather than the customary "package" units which require a central power feed with a hookup ahead of the branch circuits.

In America there are two principal church types — the cathedral or cruciform, and the wholly rectangular interior, in the spirit of the New England town meeting hall. It might be said that these represent extreme opposites, and in between the two there is a bewildering variety of physical arrangements for what one is taught to believe is a common Christian ritual of worship. We are not concerned here with theatrical in the Jewish faith, for these are invariably produced in the meeting hall rather than in the sanctuary.

In many small churches such as typified by the diagram on the preceding page, especially those with fixed piano and organ positions, with a central pulpit often permanently mounted, and with a large choir area behind the deacons' chairs, there is not much room for dramatic action, and what space there is can be difficult to light. Further, there may be very few circuits available to which portable equipment may be connected. And most certainly the cost of a central hookup would be prohibitive if there is no skilled technician at hand. In such situations I rely on a 3-tier lighting system: low-key or dim church lighting, plus sidelighting, usually with 150-watt PARs on small stands, plus a 1000-watt follow spotlight on a dimmer, from the balcony.

If there is a choice between fluorescent cove or pendant incandescent church lighting, select the latter for the low-key overall illumination. This, plus the sidelighting, should be turned on prior to the arrival of the audience and should remain on until the audience has left. The follow spotlight is used on cue. Obviously this sort of lighting lends itself to programs involving sequential scenes with readings, small choral ensembles and a minimum of stage movement. Some frontal spots such as Fresnels might be useful, but not only is there the additional power requirement but also light spill on the forward audience members is unavoidable in such a tight space. The spill from the follow spot is sufficiently distracting.

On the diagram two possible positions for the sidelights are shown, either adjacent to a column or post or masked by a small folding screen. Usually I have three PARs on a stand on each side, two with "warm" color filters and one with a "cool" filter. If enough extension cable is available, I would arrange to leave the "cools" on the entire time, while disconnecting or possibly dimming the "warms" on cue. However, the PAR units are usually connected to a single circuit, the convenience outlet for which is usually found in the pulpit or choir area.

Two electrical outlets are shown on the small church diagram. For peace of mind, these should be on separately fused circuits, for the combined load totals 1900 watts, over the capacity of a 15-amp fuse or breaker and too close for comfort for a 20-amp one. Furthermore, you might have overlooked some piece of equipment on the same circuit, such as a coke machine or drinking fountain which turns on intermittently.

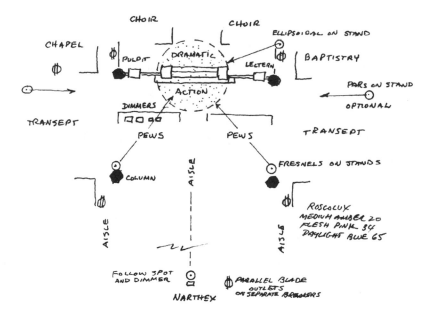

For the cruciform churches, a little knowledge of how current is distributed in the building will help. Stop by a construction site and study the fuse box on the field pole. There will probably be two "hots" and a neutral, plus a wire from the box to the ground. Then imagine this same line entering a house. Take the face plate off the panel box in the basement and study the wiring. The fuses (or circuit breakers) for most of the receptacles in the house, those to which you connect lamps, irons, radios, etc., are probably fused at 20-amperes.

Now for the church! On either side of the nave, along the walls, you will find two or more outlets. The outlets along one wall will be on one fused circuit while the outlets across the nave along the other wall will probably be fused on *another* circuit. There will be some outlets in the narthex. Also, around the lectern and pulpit. And near the altar. You must find the panel box and determine which outlets are on which breakers. Don't guess. Have an assistant connect a lamp to an outlet. Then turn off the breakers one by one until you find it. Then turn that breaker back on and have the assistant move the lamp to all the other outlets so that you can determine just which outlets are also connected to the same branch circuit. Soon you will have a diagram showing where all the outlets are and to which breakers they are connected.

Each branch circuit at 20 amps will deliver enough power to handle 2400 watts (120 volts (x) 20 amps = 2400 watts). Since you will probably be using 500-watt spots you can safely use four spots. If you had two 1000-watt dimmers you could plug them both into this circuit since the receptacle is probably duplex. Using this method of "milking" branch circuits, it is astonishing how much equipment can be connected — given a sufficient number of extension cords! Be sure you pick up all these cords after each use — it's illegal to make any permanent connections in this manner.

On the other hand, let's say you have a six-channel 2400-watt dimmer pack. This system of "milking" separate circuits won't work. Ask an electrical engineer. It's not like filling a pail with water from two hydrants. You need a suitable connection and the church must hire a licensed electrician. He will connect to terminals ahead of the circuit breakers — temporarily or permanently. For a permanent installation he might use a 60-amp range receptacle with two "hots" and a neutral. The dimmer pack will have corresponding terminals.

I always try to go a day ahead of time to identify the receptacles, circuits and fuses or breakers. If there should be a coke machine or other automatic equipment on a circuit you wish to use, check your full load with the equipment *both* starting and running. Another problem in many small churches is that the breakers are often used in lieu of switches, and some well-meaning deacon may decide to cut off your "overall dim" lighting, thinking you forgot to do it...or worse yet, fumbling around, cut off your follow spot circuit.

In the Episcopal church diagram on the preceding page where a central playing area is available and where ramps, steps and platforms are possible, the lighting by necessity must be far more ambitious and has been arranged in a different manner. Two light stands each with three 500-watt spotlights are placed adjacent to columns. A follow spot on a low stand, together with a dimmer, has been located in the narthex and aligned with the center aisle in order to cover processionals. With the angled frontal lighting a balcony follow spot is not essential and besides in the cathedral plan the balcony is usually so far away that only the more expensive follow spots will do. A backlighting of sorts has been achieved with one spot, in this instance through a perforated stone curtain wall adjacent to the baptistry.

Spotlights for the column positions are Fresnels because the soft-edged fields smooth the transition from the church illumination to the brighter dramatic area. The backlighting spot should be an ellipsoidal or a Fresnel with high hat since spill from a rear angle is not desirable. The follow spot is an 8" narrow beam 1000-watt ellipsoidal with both framing shutters and iris control, the same as used from the balcony in the preceding example.

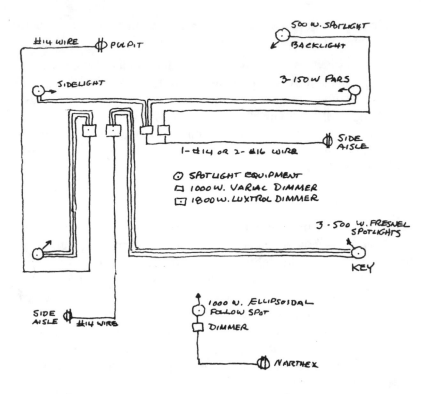

In this particular church there are eight separately fused outlets within the sanctuary proper, seven on 20-amp breakers and one on a 15-amp breaker. Of these, four are employed for this setup. A complete wiring diagram is shown on the preceding page.

Special mention must be made concerning the dimmers for the column-sited Fresnel spotlights. They are 1800-watt Luxtrol autotransformer units in homemade containers so wired that there are three output receptacles from each dimmer and one output receptacle bypassing the dimmer. This is done so that one Fresnel on each stand with a "cool" filter can be left on while the other two Fresnels with "warm" filters can be dimmed on cue. This is an excellent ploy to reduce equipment to a minimum. Eighteen hundred watts is the maximum load you can take through a 15-amp circuit. And the Luxtrol and VARIAC dimmers are used because they are autotransformer dimmers and therefore quiet, a requirement if they are to be

32

placed in the front pew, a position I like since I can use a small hand-held spotlight to touch up a scene.

One troublesome feature of this power solution is the amount of electrical cable which must be run temporarily, and most of it along the floor. Across aisles, such cables are usually taped down with silver-gray duct tape. Obviously the less bulk there is the better, so I use #16 SJ wire, save for the feeding of the 1800-watt dimmers, where #14 cable is obviously called for. And since older churches do not have grounding receptacles, most of my cables are of the 2-wire type to further reduce bulk.

In general lighting situations, the first decision for all involved concerns how much of the lighting is to be done by specialized equipment brought in and how much by equipment already in the place of the performance. The most difficult place I ever encountered was a small country church where I found, on switches, some chandeliers above the pews and some floodlights over the pulpit and choir. There was one outlet in the lobby to which a soft drink machine was attached. The only other outlet in the building was a drop cord in the minister's office back of the chancel. In addition to a bare bulb the socket had a receptacle into which the cord from the mimeograph machine was plugged.

I placed a light stand with three 150-watt PARs by one side pillar up front and a similar stand by the pillar on the other side. I connected these to the drop cord in place of the mimeograph and left the circuit on. I turned off the pulpit and choir floods but left the chandeliers on. I placed my 1000-watt follow spot with dimmer in the small balcony to the rear, running the cord down to the lobby, in place of the soft drink machine. Then I went back to the balcony and highlighted the action as best I could all the while keeping an ear cocked for a possible start-up of the soft drink machine.

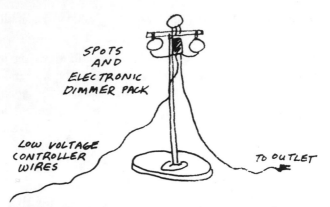

SPOTS
AND
ELECTRONIC
DIMMER PACK

LOW VOLTAGE
CONTROLLER
WIRES

TO OUTLET

A troublesome situation may develop when a director calls for a total blackout. This can be very complex, with laying on of many hands, even including those of assistants. This situation may be simplified if you are using electronic dimming with properly designed remote controllers even if you are "milking" many outlets with individual dimmers.

Technically, some of these arrangements are not strictly "code" but then this book is more of a reflection of what goes on for very practical reasons rather than what should go on under more ideal conditions. Obviously, these arrangements are of a most temporary nature, and are often excusable for that if for no other reason.

The VARIAC and Luxtrol as well as the electronic dimmers, the various stands, the making up of the PAR units, etc. are described in detail in Part II under the appropriate headings. And while the intensities of these lights may seem minimal, the question of a reasonable amount of light for these circumstances is fully discussed in the section entitled "How Much Light Do I Need?", also in Part II.

PART II
Lighting Devices and Their Uses

CHAPTER 6

How Much Light Do I Need?

Stage lighting is about lighting actors that are right before you. It is not about lighting for television or film. The latter media have exacting requirements that have little to do with the human eye in a real life situation. As was stated, the human eye is an incredible seeing machine. Since the eye is connected to a brain a viewer can recognize the artist's meaning if given half a chance.

If you like photography you probably realized a long time ago that many of your snapshots don't look much like what you thought you saw. And so it is with illumination for the living stage. It's not just a matter of so many foot candles or degrees Kelvin. All day long we walk through an incredible variety of lighting situations — involving a miscellany of sources, angles and brilliance — but as long as there are a sufficient number of highlights and contrast we don't think twice about the amount of light present or the degree of its whiteness.

Mention has been made of the proper balance between diffuse and specular light sources. Let's take the example of a restaurant when, at dinner time, all the lighting is dimmed down "a notch or two," purportedly for "intimacy," yet all that results is dullness! Add some wall sconces, table lamps and other pinpoints of light and Presto! Not only is the proper intimacy achieved but the room, while actually brighter, appears darker. We are dealing with the phenomenon of vision. In the theatre this is called "sparking a scene." When you have a tavern scene or a street scene at night, the more light that can be built into that scene the less overall lighting there needs to be. Special attention should be given to lanterns, street lamps, the glow of a drawn window shade, etc.

In the average "little theatre" situation an actor walks under 6" 500-watt Fresnel spotlights mounted on several battens about 15' above the stage. Each spotlight is probably angled downward at

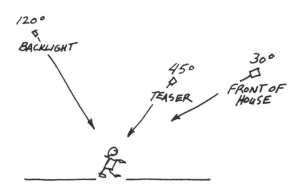

about 45° and turned sideways about 45° also, but offset in such a way that crosslighting is achieved. Thus, no matter where the actor stands, his face is crosslit by at least two spotlights — the classic McCandless setup. This works nicely with room interiors where sunlight pouring through a window suggests which spotlights have warm tinted filters, and which cool. All in all, we can safely assume that the actor will have some 40 to 50 foot candles, a very acceptable level for comedy. (The term "foot candles" here refers to reading the brilliance of illumination while standing in the subject position with an "incident light" type of photographic exposure meter pointed towards the illumination source.)

With an eye to the proper balance of lighting sources, the overall illumination may be quite dim and at the same time satisfactory for viewing purposes. With some "sparking," a cathedral nave may be as dim as 5 foot candles, yet suitable for use. With choirs present, the chancel may be as bright as 15 foot candles, and an altar is generally spotlit in some manner. Spotlights for pulpit and lectern may produce 25 foot candles. The feeling of brilliance and actual candlepower can be two very different things. Nothing is to be gained by purchasing a foot candle meter — the lighting is either acceptable or it is not, and no amount of scientific data will change that.

Data Sheets and Trade Shows

In the "old days" when things moved more slowly, lighting firms issued general catalogs. Some of these were so embellished with useful information that they were used as supplementary textbooks. Then new developments came so swiftly that the majority of the industry resorted to data sheets and trade shows; trade shows allow technicians to see products in action. The major trade show for the theatrical industry is held each March or April at rotating locations across the country. It is sponsored by the *U.S. Institute for Theatre Technology, 330 W. 42nd St., New York, NY 10036*. There are also regional theatre conferences where up-to-date wares are displayed and data sheets picked up.

A spotlight data sheet will provide the following information: the beam spread, the type of lamp, various lamps available including both wattages and color temperatures, lamp life, and charts showing foot candles at various distances. Color temperature has to do with the "whiteness" of the light and is given in Kelvin degrees. Color temperature is critical for film and television. For live theatre 2800° will be satisfactory. You will note that the higher the color temperature the shorter the life of the lamp will be. The data on foot candles is particularly important. Shown below is some information taken from a data sheet. Assuming we have the average over-the-stage mounting height of 15', I will select the upper lamp for the 52 foot candles which will give me a safe working brilliance and some 30 foot candles when a color filter and some dimming are added in.

LAMP	WATTAGE	LIFE IN HOURS	COLOR TEMP.	MAX. FOOT CANDLES		
				10'	20'	30'
500 T12/8	500	800	2800	208	52	23
500 T12/9	500	200	2900	251	83	28

"INVERSE SQUARE LAW"

39

One of the more surprising things about light is the "inverse square law" of diminishing brilliance. Once you are beyond a distance of about 10x the width of the lighting fixture or lens, the intensity of light, in theory, will fall off inversely as the square of the distance. Some particular examples are given in an extract from a spotlight performance chart. It must be realized that these figures represent relatively short "throws," so that the results are more critical than with narrower beam spotlights at greater distances.

In general, I look for 50 foot candles for the throw desired, realizing that by the time I add a color filter and perhaps dim the lamp somewhat for balancing with other light sources, I will probably end up with around 30 foot candles. Let's take a "standard" 6" ellipsoidal spotlight with a beam spread of around 35° and with a 500-watt lamp. By checking the performance data sheet (see Reading Catalogs and "Spec" Sheets) we find that a 20' throw will give us the 50 foot candles, but a 30' throw only 25 foot candles. Let's translate this in terms of a stage. The 20' throw will work nicely at a mounting height of 15' above the stage floor with the spotlight properly angled. But raise the mounting height by as little as 5' and we are in trouble. Either we must change the lamp to 750 watts, not a good idea in a 6" fixture because of heat, or substitute a spotlight with a narrower beam spread. In the case of a variable beam 500-watt Fresnel spotlight, we must either narrow the beam, change the lamp, or substitute an 8" Fresnel at 1000 watts to achieve the same illumination on stage.

What happens with brilliance when we add in more spotlights focused on the same area? Let's take a typical situation with 500-watt Fresnel spotlights on stands about 30' away, as shown in the cathedral example in Chapter 5. Here we have three spotlights atop a stand, all trained on the same area, but with different color filters. For this experiment the color filters should be removed. The first spotlight turned on produces 25 foot candles at the actor position. By adding the second, we obtain 35 foot candles. And with the third we reach 45 foot candles. Engineers call this the "waterfall" principle.

With the color filters replaced and all spots on full, we may anticipate about 30 foot candles, depending upon the degree of color saturation. And with the spotlights from the other stand across the nave added in, the scene should appear quite brilliant.

CHAPTER 7

Stage Lights and Accessories

How Spotlights Work

When one thinks of contemporary theatrical lighting it is usually in terms of spotlights. This is not because spotlights and spotlights alone produce a superior sort of dramatic illumination. They do not. A visit to any television or motion picture studio demonstrates otherwise. But the stage is not a studio. The difference is that there is an audience to be considered. And without spotlights and dimmers there would be no way to highlight important parts of a scene, not to mention the problem of stray light ("spill") which the audience sees but the studio camera does not.

The era of spotlights began in earnest with the development of a compact incandescent lamp. Early spotlights consisted of a lens and a lamp in a movable socket. By moving the socket back and forth the width of the light beam was changed (and still is in some spotlights today). A reflector was supplied though it was of dubious value except in that one position where filament and lens and reflector curvatures were complimentary to one another. These early spotlights were called "plano-convex" or PCs because this was the shape of the lens — flat on one side and bulging on the other. Lamp wattages ran from 250 to 1000 and lens diameters from three to eight inches.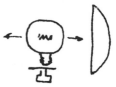

By today's standards there was not much efficiency but there was versatility with the variable focus. The beam could be softened at the color frame position by means of a photographer's sawtoothed mat or the center of a front gel removed and the remaining perimeter oiled on the dull side.

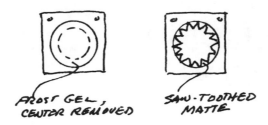

FROST GEL,
CENTER REMOVED

SAW-TOOTHED
MATTE

An objective lens system can be added for image projections. In fact, many modern effect machines still employ this light source. Perhaps the best known of these spotlights was the "baby spot" with a 4½" lens and a 400-watt G lamp, a unit that was especially popular on the small proscenium stages of the American "Little Theatre" movement of the 1920s and 1930s.

During the late 1930s the plano-convex spotlight all but disappeared in favor of two new and highly specialized spotlights: one was inherently hard-edged, the ellipsoidal reflector spotlight; the other, and inherently soft-edged, the Fresnel lens spotlight. Both are far more efficient in terms of brightness per watt, and of the two the ellipsoidal is the most efficient — and spectacularly so by the older standards. What is lost is "light all of one kind," something very noticeable when the actor approaches the curtain line and passes out from under the soft-edged illumination and into the harsher beams from the more distanced ellipsoidals mounted in the auditorium ceiling.

Lenses

The drawings below are oversimplifications of lens principles but they will serve for identification. The first lens on the left is a simple "plano-convex" and was used on all early spotlights. Today

PLANO-
CONVEX
LENS

STEP
LENS

black ceramic
on risers

FRESNEL
LENS

stippling

44

they are generally found in pairs in 6" ellipsoidal spotlights, especially when pattern templates are used.

When lenses began to be made from borosilicate glass, or "Pyrex," they could be "formed" rather than "ground," hence some intricate designs could be executed. The lens at center has excess glass removed from the rear face, thus increasing the light transmission factor. It is known as a "step" lens. The field is not as clean-edged as with the dual PCs, but one finds this type of lens with the larger diameter ellipsoidal spotlights for long throws.

To the right is another type of step lens, known by the name Fresnel, after Auguste Fresnel, a French physicist who developed this lens chiefly for lighthouse use. This lens is so designed that a light source can be placed very close, thus increasing the brilliance of the field. However, the field is rather ragged, so it is smoothed out by means of a diffusion factor in the form of stippling on the rear face. Thus the Fresnel spotlight beam is inherently soft-edged. One will often find the risers of *both* the "step" and "Fresnel" lenses fired with black ceramic, which reduces "flair." A lens so treated is said to be "co-louvred."

The design of the face of a Fresnel lens is pretty much the same from one manufacturer to another. It is on the rear face that variations occur. Generally speaking, the finer the "stippling" is the more diffuse the field will be. In the 1950s Kliegl developed, and patented, some scorings on the rear face in addition to the stippling which turned the field of a Fresnel lens from a round into an oval one, of a proportion of 3/2, a field shape useful both for "booms" and frontal washes. Unfortunately Kliegl has not offered this lens on its newer equipment since it was initially developed for use with the older tungsten filaments found in the G type lamps. Kopp Glass of Pittsburgh has a different design which performs in a similar manner, in the proportion of 2/1. The Kopp solution resembles two Fresnel lenses slightly overlapping and melted into one another with the irregular perimeter rounded off. And moving into an entirely different solution, Roscolux 104 tough Silk used in an ellipsoidal spotlight both diffuses and spreads the beam of light.

In addition to separate lenses, there are two types of lamps which have inbuilt lenses, the Rs and the PARs. The PARs are the more rugged of the two (see Homemade Equipment). With the smaller lamps one has a choice of "spot" or "flood" beams. With the larger PARs one can select either "spot," "medium flood," or "wide flood." The PAR 64s are the workhorses of rock concerts. These fields are rather ragged, but there are many technicians who prefer to work with these lamps, for with their internal reflectors they are very efficient and economical, and not everyone wants a sharp field.

The Fresnel Spotlight

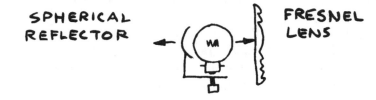

Adjustable lamp and reflector

The Fresnel spotlight is an improved version of the old plano-convex spotlight with its variable beam spread. A unique lens is employed which has greater light-gathering powers and is considerably brighter. The beam is essentially soft-edged and is ideal for blending. This lens is further described in the previous section on Lenses. The Fresnel spotlight is one of the workhorses of the studio, but its use in the theatre is limited to relatively short throws.

The Ellipsoidal Spotlight

Reflectors in the shape of half an ellipsoid were first developed by Kliegl in the 1920s for use in architectural downlighting. With this design a maximum number of rays are gathered from a carefully plotted ellipsoidal reflector. It was not long before manufacturers realized the potential of this principle as a movable fixture for dramatic lighting. However, a lamp heat problem was encountered when the architectural downlight was turned sideways. So the lamp was reinserted through the side of the reflector, thus "spoiling" the field somewhat, the missing part of the reflector causing a dim area usually right in the actor's position. To overcome this problem reflectors were "flatted" and double "flatted." But in the 1960s a new type of lamp was developed with quartz rather than glass so that a proper axial mounting was again possible and the field greatly improved.

ORIGINAL
DOWNLIGHT

TUNGSTEN
LAMPED

AXIALLY
MOUNTED
"QUARTZ"

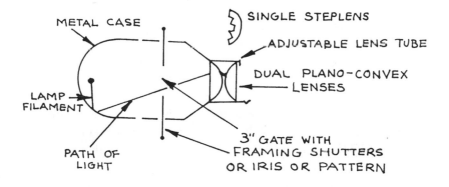

METAL CASE

SINGLE STEPLENS

ADJUSTABLE LENS TUBE

DUAL PLANO-CONVEX
LENSES

LAMP
FILAMENT

PATH OF
LIGHT

3" GATE WITH
FRAMING SHUTTERS
OR IRIS OR PATTERN

Light gathering and the consequent brilliance is but one of the desirable features of ellipsoidal spotlights. Another feature is that the light passes through a small aperture called the "gate," about three inches in diameter. It is in this plane that the profiles of any objects appear sharply defined in the light beam. Thus we can have shaping or matting shutters which mask out the proscenium frame with razor sharp definition, or an iris shutter for a follow spot oper

47

ation, or one of the myriad patterns or "templates" which provide inexpensive background decoration. In effect, the ellipsoidal spotlight is the projector of sorts.

Countering these very desirable features is a spotlight that, in its basic design form, has an essentially hard-edged beam. This hard edge makes blending difficult though this can be mitigated somewhat by racking the lens system slightly out of focus or using some of the new Rosco diffusion filters. The ellipsoidal is essentially a fixed spread instrument although, within limits, there are possible lens changes. And recent developments include some variable focus (zoom) lenses.

Ellipsoidals of the narrow-beam spreads are essential for the long throws from auditorium ceilings and outdoor stage lighting towers. Wide-angled ellipsoidals are useful for sidelighting, especially for dance. And some lighting designers prefer them over Fresnels because of the precise control although this use may involve some diffusion techniques. Roscolux 101 Light Frost and 110 Matte Diffusion filters will help.

In analyzing ellipsoidal data sheets, one should assume that the published foot candle readings are taken at the center of the beam when the field is "peaked" rather than "flatted." A peak field is one where the lamp and reflector are adjusted to produce the brightest possible beam center. A flat field is one where the overall field is even though it may be somewhat dimmer. By definition the beam angle is established at that diameter where the fall off does not exceed 50 percent of the beam center reading, while the field angle extends to 10 percent of the center reading. With the older incandescent type ellipsoidals this adjustment is time consuming. With the newer axially mounted lamps, the adjustment is simpler so this option is mentioned more often.

Floodlights

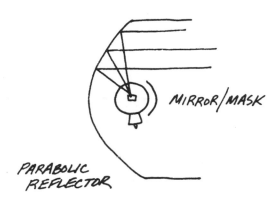

THE BEAM LIGHT

MIRROR/MASK

PARABOLIC REFLECTOR

The above floodlight goes by a variety of names such as a beam projector, a beam light, a narrow-beam floodlight and, in England, a pageant lantern. Some might call it a Klieg for this is the principle by which powerful searchlights are designed. Since no lens is involved, light output per watt is considerably higher than for spotlights. The usual theatrical model has a 10" polished parabolic reflector and a 1000-watt lamp. On stage they are useful for back-lighting, sidelighting and strong accent lighting. Used from offstage with box sets they create very convincing shafts of sunlight or moonlight pouring through windows. They are also very useful in outdoor theatres as a primary source of illumination.

There are definite advantages to this sort of illumination, especially where the stage floor is a highly visible part of the overall background, and where the sharp edges of ellipsoidal spotlight beams would be distracting, the throw distances exceeding those practical with Fresnel lens spotlights. If in some sort of artistic Valhalla, I would be limited to one type of stage lighting fixture for all time, my choice would be the beam light.

The Scoop

Scoops are used for flooding cycloramas and other backgrounds. They provide a very diffuse, even illumination. A typical scoop is shown below.

Alzak etched aluminum (matte finish) ellipsoidal reflector

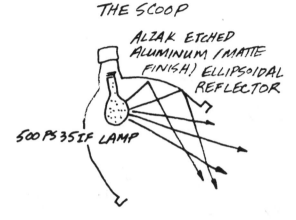

In general, the more diffuse floodlights in the theatre are in a stage of disrepair. The old "x-ray" large compartment borderlights began disappearing during the 1940s, being replaced by tightly centered PAR and R reflector lamps. Footlights went out when thrust stages came in. And the old traditional "scoop" as shown above, becomes scarcer every day, pushed aside by "Quartz" fever.

Since the traditional scoop is absolutely essential for my background projection system, the "quartz" lamped scoops tending to "hotspot" when partially dimmed, I am taking some pains to show the design and lamping of a proper scoop. The lamp must be the pear-shaped, inside-frosted type. A clear lamp will not work, nor will a quartz lamp even though it may be frosted. Nor should the lamp be adjustable.

Color Media

Once, colored light was obtained by dipping electric lamps into transparent lacquer dyes. This method is no longer practical with lamps over 40 watts due to increased lamp efficiency and with this an attendant heat problem. These dyes are still available, however, and are useful for low wattage lamps in open front backing strips behind doorways, etc. The chief use of these dyes today is in the preparation of translucent imagery for light projections. Olesen and Kliegl still stock the original dyes. And Rosco has added a similar line designed especially for transparent imagery.

The next color filters consisted of dyed gelatine sheets, commonly called "gels." The best known supplier then was the Brigham Gelatine Company and their color nomenclature was a "textbook" standard through the 1930s and into the early 1940s. But as both lamp wattages and spotlight efficiency increased the gelatine filters gave way to the acetates, the Cinemoids and Roscolenes, and these in turn gave way to the polyesters such as Roscolux, these being the only bases which can stand up to the tremendous heat from the new "quartz" lamps. However, the term "gel" has become generic and now refers to all manner of color media placed in front of spotlights and floods.

It is virtually impossible to match up colors from one base and brand to another and designers must learn by experience what colors are good within a line. Brigham's Special Lavender 17 has never been equalled for bringing out the best in female flesh tones. Cinemoid's Pale Green 38 is unbelievably excellent for lighting actors in a moonlight scene. The late Gilbert Helmsley used Roscolux 105 Tough Spun for a diffuse hot center and overall dim spread, his "kerosene light special." Furthermore, each age seems to have had a preference for a certain kind of "look" to the stage. In the late 1920s amber was considered a mark of theatricality. Even into the 1950s people from remote country locations seeking "gels" would ask for amber first. Rock concerts are known for their use of heavily saturated colors.

It must also be remembered that with the human eye a relationship of colors is frequently more significant than the color itself. For example, if an actor is lit from four different directions with bluish tints of different values, the tint nearest a gray-blue will appear "warm" rather than the "cool" tint it really is. Try this experiment with Roscolux 60, 61, 62 and 63. Furthermore, with the human eye, a heavily saturated color on a background such as a cyclorama, though less bright than a lighter color, will *appear* brighter and provide a more satisfactory color sensation.

When lamps are dimmed the color temperature or "whiteness" of the filaments is lowered, that is, they become yellower, thus changing the color values of the filters, the "cools" being the more adversely affected. This is why you cannot make "all the colors of the rainbow" by blending the light primaries of red, blue and green with those heavily saturated glass roundels used on so many borderlight strips. That dimming plays havoc with color filters any production photographer knows only too well and in studios dimming is avoided if possible. Fortunately, live audiences do not know how bad things really are. Inbuilt into their perception of reality is a phenomenon known to scientists as "the persistence of vision." There are, however, certain color filters that can be brightened or dimmed without an appreciable change of color hue: Roscolux Pale Yellow 07, Daylight Blue 65 and Chocolate 99.

Most professional designers have light closets where spotlights are set up with preferred color filters, usually those which work well with the human face. In these "dark rooms" portions of painted scenery and costume fabrics are tested for compatibility with the future lighting. In a commercial operation it is very costly to have to change color filters at the last minute. In the boondocks such careful coordination is often absent, so a good rule of thumb is to use only the lightest tints from spotlights mounted in frontal positions. Save the more saturated colors for the sides, rear obliques, backlighting and downlighting.

Diffusion

Already mentioned is the difference between specular and diffuse sources of light, and the difficulty of getting a proper blend of these sources on stage. Around the turn of the century Mariano Fortuny attempted to create diffuse lighting for the stage by bouncing very bright light off colored silks. Though this proved impractical in the theatre, strikingly similar methods are employed every day in television and motion pictures. And the white silk parasol virtually has become the trademark of the photographer's studio!

Obviously there is no room for reflector panels and such when live audiences are present. For that matter, space is so limited in theatre that such ersatz sources of diffuse lighting as scoops, footlights, box floodlights and the large compartment-type borderlights (affectionately known as "X-rays" to old-timers) are difficult to mount; and in some theatres, particularly the thrust and the arena, there are no diffuse sources — it's spotlights or nothing! Hence the welcome news of the new Rosco diffusion filters.

Can one conclude that the theatre is full of bad lighting? One might, but for one thing — the way the human eye works, as opposed to the eye of a camera. The human eye transfers bits of visual information, piecemeal, to the mind, letting the memory assist with the construction of the mental imagery. The actor may feel that he is in a police station being grilled under lights which preclude the identity of his inquisitors, but the audience does not. Amazingly superb imagery can be created in the audience's mind by spotlights alone, but there are definite technical drawbacks.

For one thing, age is not masked by specular lighting. For another, there is the matter of shadows. Each specular source creates a clear shadow. Several are fine, but a great many shadows on the floor and on the scenery confuse the eye and distract the attention. Yet another problem is the blending of purely specular sources into a smooth continuity of illumination through which the actor moves.

Establishing a proper diffuse base of illumination lessens the impact of these drawbacks listed above. In the section on Lighting Chancel Drama, the overall church illumination at a low level of brilliance can be considered a rather diffuse base. In the section on the High School Auditorium, the base illumination was supplied by the Fresnel spotlights, some with oval beam lenses for maximum spread. And in the section on Lighting for Little Theatres the footlights, large compartment-type borderlights and just plain old box floods on stands help.

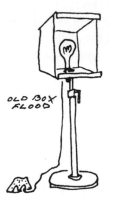

Fresnel lenses, by design, create shafts of light that are essentially soft-edged, some more than others depending upon the nature of the etching or stippling on the rear surface of the lens. Ellipsoidal spotlights normally produce sharp-edged beams, though these can be softened somewhat by racking the lens slightly out of focus at the expense of a less even field. A more efficient way to soften these fields is by use of the new Roscolux diffusion filters. Some of these are:

101 Light Frost	Turns an ellipsoidal spotlight into a Fresnel.
110 Matte Diffusion	Turns an ellipsoidal spotlight into a Fresnel, with a slight oval spread.
104 Tough Silk	Spreads light, and especially useful for sidelighting.
105 Tough Spun	Gilbert Helmsley's "kerosene light special," which produces a diffuse hot center and an overall dim spread.

As with any other aspect of lighting, each designer has his own techniques which work well for him, and perhaps for no one else. Each age, too, seems to have its own idea of how the stage should look. The early lighting of the Canadian Stratford Festival Stage employed parabolic beam projectors (the British "pageant lantern") which produced shafts of soft-edged light. On the other hand, the lighting in the newer Tyrone Guthrie Festival Stage in Minneapolis uses a vast assemblage of ellipsoidal spotlights which creates some very distracting patterns on the floor.

Clamps for Lights

Undoubtedly the mounting of equipment by standard C-clamps is preferred over any other method of attachment chiefly because the clamp, once hooked over a pipe, supports the weight of the equipment while the bolt is tightened down. You can even do this with one hand while hanging onto a ladder with the other. With Unistrut and extruded aluminum plugging strips you have to hold the yoke steady while you fit the bolt into the spring-loaded nut or sliding bar, something that is best done with three hands.

On a lighting catwalk a 1½" pipe guard rail is customary for mounting lighting equipment. The clearance between such a pipe and the catwalk deck is critical when the equipment is to hang directly below the pipe. For most 6" spotlights, both Fresnel and ellipsoidal, and for 8" Fresnel spotlights, 24" is usually sufficient clearance between the underside of the pipe rail and the deck framing. For larger spotlights and for 14" scoops 30" will be necessary. These measurements include the use of standard C-clamps. Where the rail is made of Unistrut (Unistrut Corp., 35005 Michigan Avenue West, Wayne, MI 48184) or of extruded aluminum plugging strips, the yoke is bolted directly to the mounting device and the C-clamp is not used. Thus, 4" can be subtracted from the above clearances.

However, certain mounting problems are encountered with lighting catwalks that do not occur where lights are hung from rigged battens or mounting strips. The catwalk deck gets in the way of downlighting, crosslighting and backlighting. This calls for the spotlight to be offset from the basic mounting device. It must also be remembered that for universal adjustment the spotlight yoke must be absolutely vertical. For pipe rails, a standard arm such as the Olesen 29130 type will suffice for purely horizontal offsetting. For Unistrut or other slotted devices, a number of ¼" flat metal strips drilled with bolt holes will suffice. However, simple offsetting is not always the answer. It may be necessary to simultaneously off-

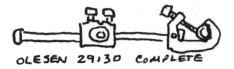

OLESEN 29130 COMPLETE

set and lower the spotlight, especially where lighting ports occur in double-plated auditorium ceilings, and this calls for more sophisticated mounting equipment. Two solutions are sketched out below. One must also bear in mind that these adjustable hangers will distance the spotlights farther from fixed plugging receptacles and the customary 3' leads which are furnished with most lighting equipment will not suffice. I usually specify 6' leads.

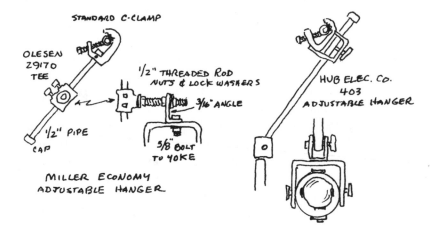

Shown on the following page is a standard stage tree with side arms for the mounting of spotlights, usually for wing positions for crosslighting. Such spotlights are often referred to as "booms." With the exception of the C-clamp and the sliding tee, parts to make similar but inexpensive trees can be obtained locally. See the section on Homemade Equipment for the construction of pipe and base, but use 1¼" or 1½" pipe instead. There are usually spare C-clamps around since they are included in factory-packed spotlight cartons whether you order them or not. I am told that it costs more to reopen these cartons and remove the clamps than the clamps are worth. You will need to order the sliding tee separately. Then you will need about 18" of ½"

pipe (¾" o.d.), threaded at both ends, and also two caps per arm. The pipe substitutes for the short stem which comes with the C-clamp.

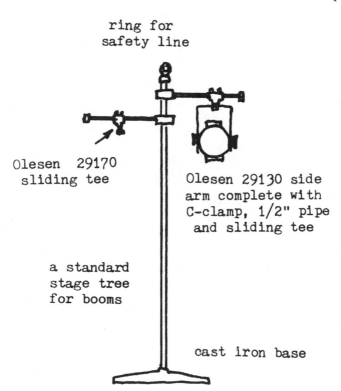

ring for
safety line

Olesen 29170
sliding tee

Olesen 29130 side
arm complete with
C-clamp, 1/2" pipe
and sliding tee

a standard
stage tree
for booms

cast iron base

See Homemade Equipment for a less expensive version of a spotlight stand.

One of the most frustrating experiences is attempting to use a C-clamp for attachment to shapes other than a pipe, as for example to the tread of a stepladder. So some years back I had the Hub Electric Co. design a lightweight clamp that can be converted to board or pipe attachment. I use these clamps for the small 10" floods for backings.

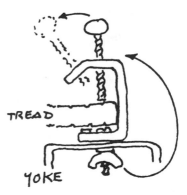

TREAD

YOKE

CHAPTER 8

Dimmers and Cues

Dimmers

In theatrical parlance, "dimmers" are the devices which alter the current supply to lamp filaments, thus making it possible to adjust the brightness of lighting fixtures. Dimmers are essential for three reasons: to balance the various light sources of a scene in a pleasing and meaningful way, to change lighting levels in a manner that is not distracting, and to be able to pass smoothly from one scene to another.

The subject of theatrical dimming is a complex one, thus often confusing to the layman. The simplest form of all dimming is that of resistance (a rheostat) where an adjustable resistor is so constructed that its resistance may be changed without opening the circuit. It might be likened to an adjustable toaster because the unwanted current is drawn off in heat, or, in a water analogy, the cutting of holes in a garden hose to prevent the full pressure from reaching the nozzle. Today resistance dimming, once necessary for direct current, has been largely superseded, but the principle would be quite satisfactory for our needs here.

With the advent of alternating current the most reliable dimmer has been the autotransformer. Simply stated, an autotransformer dimmer is one which has a single winding around a silicon steel core. A mechanical slider passes over an exposed portion of the winding, tapping off the voltage desired. A water analogy would be decreasing the flow of water by turning the faucet. Although an autotransformer is a heavy object and basically a manual controller, it is inherently silent and free of radio interference, important points when you consider the portable dimmers are often right in the audience and adjacent to portable sound equipment.

Another type of dimmer is the silicon controlled rectifier, consisting of a pair of rectifiers, one for each half-cycle of the alternating current. The "SCR" is basically a switching device. A transistorized pilot circuit controls the length of time the switch is open during the "on" period of each rectifier. In a water analogy each of the pairs of rectifiers may be said to produce spurts of water, the duration of the spurts being variable.

The analogy also points up the fact that the "SCR" operates by "chopping" into the characteristic wave pattern of alternating current. This "chopping," unless smoothed out by proper filters, chokes and capacitors, produces *radio frequency* interference and *lamp sing,* that is, sound interference and mechanical vibrations in lamp filaments. The chief advantage of "SCR" dimming is the simplicity of low voltage remote controllers which, when hooked to electronic memory systems, eliminate the old hand-written cue sheets and, in large installations, even the cumbersome "patch" panels for the grouping of circuitry. Also, the low voltage control wires can be freely strung about, thus making the remote control of separately located light stands possible.

There are some factors to be considered on the down side of electronic dimming. First, there is an inherent voltage drop over full line voltage. This is caused by the various filters, chokes and capacitators which "smooth" wave forms distortion. About three percent of full line voltage is lost and the color temperature and candlepower specified for lamp filaments are not achieved. Of course, this drop could be compensated by booster transformers but this is not economically viable in a competitive market. In large installations this drop can be offset somewhat by adding more lighting units. But in our "Poor Richard" operation every bit of brilliance is important.

Second, there is no way to walk around the cost of a properly filtered electronic dimmer. Off-the-shelf hardware store dimmers for home lighting fixtures are not reliable unless permanently wired into a circuit. Plugging fixtures into such a dimmer that is already turned on (known as "hot patching" in the theatrical trade) will usually cause the dimmer to fail (and, by the way, this is also true of autotransformer dimmers, which damages the coil contacts). Further, these little dimmers can create static which feeds back into sound equipment. Try using your cordless telephone with your dining room chandelier turned on, or plug a radio into a nearby outlet.

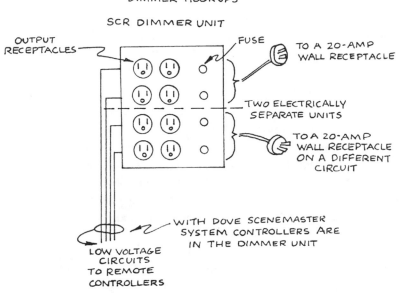

TYPICAL PORTABLE WALL OUTLET
DIMMER HOOKUPS

SCR DIMMER UNIT

OUTPUT RECEPTACLES

FUSE

TO A 20-AMP WALL RECEPTACLE

TWO ELECTRICALLY SEPARATE UNITS

TO A 20-AMP WALL RECEPTACLE ON A DIFFERENT CIRCUIT

WITH DOVE SCENEMASTER SYSTEM CONTROLLERS ARE IN THE DIMMER UNIT

LOW VOLTAGE CIRCUITS TO REMOTE CONTROLLERS

Given these reservations, there are some properly filtered electronic systems that are designed for the 20-amp wall outlet hookup method. While one hesitates to list sources in a manual that might just outlast specific manufacturers in a volatile marketplace, I'll give several that are valid for 1989: Dove Systems of San Luis Obispo, California, particularly the Scenemaster I with 1000-watt dimmers; LSS Laboratories of Wallingford, Connecticut, with their M-3000 dimmer pack designed for small bands and clubs; and Grand Stage Co. of Chicago, Illinois, with their Warrior 412 and Procon II Control Console.

When you consider that resistance dimming is so reliable that dimmers have frequently outlasted the buildings they were installed in, and that with proper care autotransformer dimming is nearly as reliable, one might well ask, "Why the trade-off for electronic dimming?" The answer is simple: superb control. Electronic dimmers respond to remotely located, miniaturized controllers which work on low voltage. Not only are numerous presets possible at a very low cost, but cues can also be fed directly into electronic memory banks, eliminating the old hand-scripted cue sheets and often

61

bypassing the controllers entirely. Also eliminated are the laying on of many hands although miniaturized controllers make very subtle adjustments difficult. But electronic dimming is here to stay and resistance and autotransformer dimmers are pretty much things of the past. And in rock concerts and disco lighting, electronic systems are absolutely essential.

There is no point in purchasing electronic dimmers, however, unless you acquire all the features which make electronic dimming worth having, such as a control console which features independent as well as preset dimmer options, masters and cross-faders, and a timed cross-fader, the latter being a feature which can restore a little of the subtlety that is lost when a human hand tries to move a miniaturized controller very slowly. The do-it-yourselfer must also be warned against the sort of electronic dimmers which can be substituted for all switches in domestic wiring. Not only are these not filtered, but they are not designed to be used for circuitry other than permanently connected loads such as chandeliers and wall brackets. In theatrical practice, loads are frequently connected after a dimmer has been turned on, a practice known as "hot patching," and these inexpensive household dimmers will likely fail if "hot patched." Usually there are instructions inside their packing boxes which so state. And regarding the selection of a "memory" electronic dimmer system, one should inquire as to the number of "steps" or distinct output levels. For example, most Kliegl dimmers employ 100 "steps," which will produce a sufficient number of readings for any situation however subtle.

With this "advanced state of the art" one might think there is no further need for the other types of dimmers. This is not so. There are many small groups who can manage nicely with manual boards and who could not afford the maintenance of an electronic system even if such service were readily available. Then there are those artists who like to have some freedom in adjusting their lighting cues as the show goes on rather than relying entirely on prearranged cues which may or may not be in rhythm with a particular performance. This "free-style" sort of lighting control works better if the controllers are *not* miniaturized, and if there are not too many of them. Some operators even prefer the dial-type autotransformer control for the rearranging of intensities in such a subtle manner that the audience remains unaware of any mechanical adjustments being made.

At this time of writing, the purchase of resistance dimmers is pretty much a thing of the past, though you will still find these reliable dimmers in constant use in many Broadway shows. Autotransformers were the mainstay of most institutional lighting installations from the 1930s through the 1960s until the widespread use of electronic control in industry made solid-state dimming competitive in price. And while autotransformers are no longer routinely listed in theatrical supply catalogs, both factory-made packages and individual parts are still available. Write the Superior Electric Co., Bristol, CT 06010 for catalogs of both their Luxtrol line and their Powerstat variable transformers. Also write GenRad, 300 Baker Ave., Concord, MA 01742 for a catalog listing their VARIAC Continually Adjustable Autotransformers. Those making up their own boards will find the "W" types useful. Another useful type is their "WMT," a dimmer in a case with carrying handle complete with input and output connections and breaker protection. I use the W10MT3 unit for both church theatricals and small touring situations.

When autotransformer dimmers were plentiful the dial types could be built into small wooden carrying cases and items such as fuses, output receptacles, plugs, cords and wires added from readily available shelf items in local building supply stores. There are still some stockpiles of dimmers used in the repair of autotransformer dimmers. Contact Vara-Light/Dimmatronics of Crystal Lake, Illinois.

Superior Electric Co. of Bristol, Connecticut still manufactures wall box dimmers for commercial installations such as restaurants, etc. The 800-watt (for use with a 750-watt followspot) and the 1800-watt units are useful. Below is the 1800-watt unit boxed for travel and showing my own arrangement of additional circuitry.

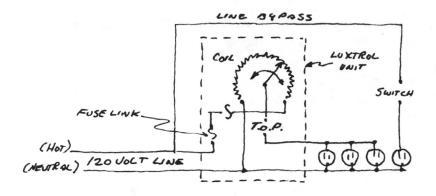

For individual use such as we are doing here it doesn't matter which way the plug is inserted in a wall outlet. But if you were installing this unit in a building you would follow instructions and identify the hot and neutral wires.

In most autotransformer dimmers the manufacturer inserts a fuse link as a protective device of last resort. Such links are available from the factory only. Usually the dimmer should be returned to the factory for servicing when this link breaks, but a qualified electrician or a knowledgeable do-it-yourselfer may be able to make this repair in the field once the proper link is obtained. The symbol "S" is a switch which opens automatically when the knob reaches the completely dimmed down position. This is a feature found on wall box dimmers only. "T.O.P." stands for thermal overload protector, which automatically cycles the lights "off" and "on" if the dimmer is overloaded, or remains "off" if there is a short in a lighting fixture or cord. Immediately disconnect dimmer and all circuitry. Test each cord and fixture and ascertain the trouble before reconnecting. The encased Variac dimmers have a manual reset breaker button which serves the same purpose.

The illustration on the following page shows the Superior 1800-watt wall box dimmer mounted to ½" plywood which is recessed against ¾" x 4" cleats.

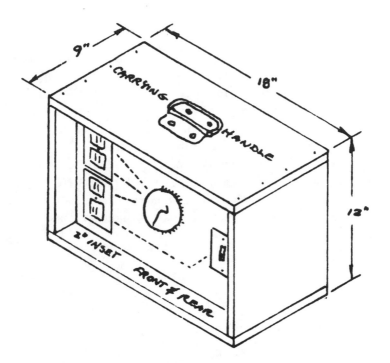

In addition to Superior Electric, the old VARIAC adjustable autotransformers are now manufactured by Technipower of Danbury, Connecticut. These are designed chiefly for laboratory use and are individually packaged, complete with output receptacle, input cable and plug, and a protective fusing. All in all, allow about $1,000 for dimmer needs, including homemade cases and parts.

Portable Dimmers on the Move

Frequently, a technician finds himself trying to connect some lights in a school gymnasium, in a fellowship hall or on some concert platform. So a little knowledge of how current is distributed in the building will help. Stop by a construction site and study the fuse box on the field pole. There will probably be two "hots" and a neutral, plus a wire from the box to the ground. Then imagine this same line entering a house. Take the face plate off the panel box in the basement and study the wiring. The fuses (or circuit breakers) for most of the receptacles in the house, those to which you connect lamps, irons, radios, etc. are probably fused at 20 amperes.

Now for the boondocks situations in schools, churches, etc. Along the walls, you will find two or more outlets. The outlets along one wall will be on one fused circuit while the outlets along the other wall will probably be fused on *another* circuit. You must find the panel box and determine which outlets are on which breakers. Don't guess. Have an assistant connect a lamp to an outlet. Then turn off the breakers one by one until you find it. Then turn that breaker back on and have the assistant move the lamp to all the other outlets so that you can determine just which outlets are also connected to the same branch circuit. Soon you will have a diagram showing where all the outlets are and to which breakers they are connected.

Each branch circuit at 20 amps will deliver enough power to handle 2400 watts (120 volts (x) 20 amps = 2400 watts). Since you will probably be using 500-watt spots you can safely use four spots. You could then plug two 1000-watt dimmers into each circuit since the receptacle is probably duplex. Using this method of "milking" branch circuits, it is astonishing how much equipment can be connected — given a sufficient number of extension cords! Be sure you pick up all these cords after each use — it's illegal to make any permanent connections in this manner.

On the other hand, let's say you have a six-channel 2400-watt dimmer pack. This system of "milking" separate circuits won't work. Ask an electrical engineer. It's *not* like filling a pail with water from two hydrants. You need a suitable connection and must hire a licensed electrician. He will connect to terminals ahead of the circuit breakers — temporarily or permanently. For a permanent installation he might use a 60-amp range receptacle with two "hots" and a neutral. The dimmer pack will have corresponding terminals.

It's also astonishing just how much equipment there is to be had based on the concept of "milking" 20-amp circuits for small theatres, studios, clubs and touring groups. And while it is always chancey to list specific sources in a book, the following have electronic dimmer packs designed specifically for this situation:

66

Show Trol International   LSS Laboratories, Inc.
2220 Shorecrest Drive   P.O. Box 866
Dallas, TX 75235   Wallingford, CT 06492

Patch Panels

Patch panels, also known as cross-connect or plugging panels, are devices often inserted between permanently installed dimmer banks and branch circuits for the purpose of making connections between dimmers and stage lights rearrangeable.

There are two reasons for using patch panels. The first has to do with consolidating control in terms of particular cues so that an operator does not have to find a number of widely separated dimmer handles for a particular lighting sequence. The second has to do with using a small number of dimmers to best advantage, assuming that all branch circuits will not be loaded simultaneously.

With resistance and autotransformer dimmers that are manually controlled a patch panel is indispensable. With electronic dimmers and controllers that can be preset the importance of a patch panel diminishes as the number of dimmers increase, and, with a sufficient number of dimmers, plus memory assist, a patch panel becomes unnecessary.

One doesn't find patch panels as such with portable touring systems since the portable dimmer boards are, in effect, flexible patch panels themselves and further flexibility can be had through the use of multiple receptacle boxes. Here, the circuitry is *not* permanent and is plugged in as desired for a particular production. A somewhat parallel situation occurs with the use of electronic dimmer packs located at intervals in a theatre where the lighting system is serviced by catwalks. There, short cables are used between the dimmer packs and adjacent lights. The dimmer packs are then operated by low voltage control cables by remote controllers at some centralized location.

There are two types of cross-connected or "patch" panels, the plug-in and the cross-grid matrix. With the plug-in, the hot side of each branch circuit terminates in a flexible cord with pin-plug cap which can be inserted into a selected dimmer output receptacle. Each dimmer has a number of these output receptacles depending upon its capacity. With the cross-grid matrix, two sets of parallel conductor bars are set at right angles to one another, with space between. Interconnections are made between them as desired. An early connector was in the form of a slotted metal device with an insulated handle, hence the name "clothespin" panel for that particular design. More recently, spring-loaded sliders have been used which make contact when the handle is "backed up" and a spring pressure released.

It is, of course, possible to overload a dimmer with the plug-in type, but since there is a limited number of receptacles per dimmer and the process is a visual one, the chances for overloading are considerably diminished. Not so with the cross-grid matrix. On many it is possible to load every circuit in the stage lighting system onto one dimmer with subsequent dimmer damage despite the protective breakers. And with the slider type cross-grid matrix it is chancey to rearrange the circuitry during the running of a show, that is, to slide past unwanted connections without accidentally touching upon them, and to know for sure that a slider is properly seated upon the desired circuit bar.

Cues

The word *cue* comes from the old script abbreviation "q" for Latin *quando* or *when*, and in stage lighting indicates a change of illumination. But while the definition seems simple enough there is nothing so troublesome in stage lighting as the business of cues. All too often an unholy triangle is created between the demands of a playwright or director, those who must plan and execute the cues and the nature of the control equipment available.

Cues may range anywhere from instantaneous rearrangements of nearly all the lighting sources and their intensities such as those for *A Chorus Line* to long gathering dusk scenes such as the fourteen-minute sequence which concludes the first act of the opera *Butterfly*. A preset electronic control system with a memory bank would be essential for *A Chorus Line*, whereas the very slow-paced string of cues that are normally involved in the *Butterfly* scene could probably be best done with a rack of dial-type autotransformer dimmers. However, in art, there are many solutions to the same ends and, with few exceptions, dimming equipment is used because it is available rather than being selected for a particular production.

The matter of cues is touched on briefly in the section on Dimmers, in the discussion of different types of dimmers and the nature of their operation. An especially critical problem with electronic dimming is the more complex cue with overlapping sequences in both ascending and descending brilliances that are running at different rates of speed. When electronic dimming was first introduced the engineering for it was chiefly in terms of scene-to-scene sequences. If a cue came up within a scene, it was considered a "sub-scene," and a change within that, a "sub-sub-scene," and so forth. But this sort of thinking did not come to grips with the overlapping type of cue, and even now only the most advanced kind of electronic boards address themselves to this problem. On the other hand, total rearrangements of lighting, simultaneously done, which before had been virtually impossible with any degree of sophistication on the manual boards, are "duck soup" for the most basic electronic board with a two-scene preset capability.

Cue sheet formats are largely a matter of individual preference. With hand-scripted sheets I prefer a style which not only indicates changes but displays complete dimmer readings between changes on cue. This simplifies corrections and also backing up or jumping from scene to scene during rehearsals.

With many new electronic dimmers which interface with memory control systems the old handwritten cue sheets may be eliminated. When a scene is lit to satisfaction during a rehearsal, a recording button is pushed and the cues drop into the memory, sequentially numbered. The mark of a good control system of this type is how the system reacts to "changes of mind," not only in redoing the cue for memory but in altering it in a subtle manner during performance. Also additional cues may have to be inserted between those already sequenced. Without features which can handle these operations, the desirability of these systems is questionable.

CHAPTER 9

The Nature of Power Hookups

In order to hook up the feed cables from any portable board whose total output exceeds 2400 watts (and thus not able to be connected to an ordinary wall outlet protected by a 20-amp fuse or breaker), it will be necessary to know something about how power is supplied. The best way to begin an explanation is with an example that is highly visible, such as a roadside electrical service pole as shown in the sketch below. It will also be helpful to look at a contractor's pole and service box used at construction sites.

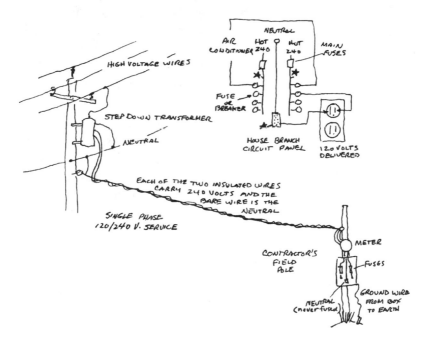

Shown just above this sketch is a typical household service box containing fuses or breakers for the branch circuits. With the exception of electric stoves and most air conditioners, each branch circuit is completed by connecting from a "hot" to the "neutral," thereby delivering 120 volts for light fixtures and household appliances. Lamps in most theatrical equipment are also designed to operate at a maximum of 120 volts. There is a popular misconception in the theatre that a higher voltage is required because the electrical cables appear bigger than household extension cords. They are bigger, for the amperage, that is, the amount of current being carried, is greater, though the voltage remains the same.

On the house branch circuit panel on page 71 there are three "stars." If you were trying to hook up the multiple receptacle box shown at the conclusion of this section, these "stars" would be likely contact spots for the "hots" and the "neutral" feed wires. There would be no problem in hooking up such a receptacle box in theatres or hotel exhibition areas, but poking around in service closets in churches and the like in the boondocks is quite another matter. Preferably the owner, his electrical contractor, or one of his maintenance staff should make the hookup under your close supervision. Poking leads under the lugs of internal feed cables in wall panels is a dangerous practice and liable to lead to inadvertent overloading.

For most ordinary situations in the boondocks we could stop right here, for when larger hookups are encountered there are bound to be professional electricians about. However, a little general knowledge won't hurt. On the service pole diagram is the statement "single phase 120/240 service." This refers to the "two hots and a neutral" type of service. Another statement often encountered will be "four-wire three-phase 120/208 service." This means that there will be three "hots" and one "neutral." The 208 refers to voltage delivered between any two "hots," a situation that does not apply to our needs here. The Kliegpac 9 is unique among portable dimmer packages in that it requires this type of service and does not adapt well to a "single phase" connection. Most other portable dimmer packages on the market have six dimmers and these can be rewired internally for either type of connection as per instructions which come with the packages.

In any hookup the neutral lead wire must always go to the neutral connection. This is inviolate. The "neutral" wire concept is an economy measure. Not only does it simplify the delivery of electricity but normally the neutral does not have to carry much current, thus saving on a considerable amount of wire. In the diagram, if each lamp is of the same wattage, and if they are both turned on simultaneously, the neutral carries no current at all.

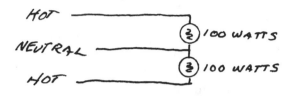

An electrical engineer attempts to design into an installation in a building as many loads as possible that will tend to balance themselves out. In the theatre, loads are more frequently unbalanced, and neutrals are planned for more current capacity. Neutrals are *never* fused and this is one way by which they can be identified. Always check neutrals for tight connections, for some pretty strange things can happen when a neutral connection is broken. A telltale sign of a loose neutral is when some spotlights being dimmed up cause other spotlights to change their brightness level.

In any hookup one should be concerned with the current carrying capacities of the wires involved. For example, the Kliegpac 9 requires a four-wire three-phase 60 ampere service. This means three "hots" *each* fused at 60 amps. There are three 2400-watt dimmers on each phase or "hot."

$$3 \times 2400 = \frac{7200 \text{ watts}}{120 \text{ volts}} = 60 \text{ amps}$$

A #4 wire is called for. In the case of our multiple receptacle box we have four duplex receptacles, each fused at 20 amps. There are two "hot" leads, thus each lead should be able to carry 40 amps. This would ordinarily call for a #6 wire. However, this particular box was designed for a road tour operation using 500- and 1000-watt spotlights only. Therefore, each circuit would never be called upon to deliver 2400 watts, but 2000 maximum instead.

$$\frac{4000 \text{ watts}}{120 \text{ volts}} = 33.3 \text{ amps}$$

Thus a #8 gauge wire (usually rated at 35 amps) would be adequate.

There is yet one subject to be covered, and that is "grounding." The newer electrical codes require it. "Grounding" is connecting the equipment itself to the earth, so that any internal connection which comes loose and electrifies the metal case of a spotlight, plugging strip or dimmer box does not attempt to ground itself through a worker. Despite the fact that the neutral is grounded at frequent intervals, the neutral and ground wires are not identical in function. When loads are unbalanced one can get quite a shock from a neutral.

Ordinarily, when making up a simple extension cord for connecting up a spotlight you will probably be using a cord with three wires each with insulation of a different color — black for hot, white for neutral, and green for ground. *This color coding does not necessarily apply to feed cables.* You might find yourself using a heavy-duty three-wire feed cable with black, white and green colors going to a three-wire single-phase service box. In this case, the black and white might go to the "hots" and the green to the "neutral." The grounding of the dimmer box may have been accomplished in another way. Thus, one cannot go by color alone, but must *positively* identify all the wires of a feed cable at *both* ends, or have them properly tagged.

Earlier I mentioned the "raw" power always available for hookups in civic auditoriums and commercial roadhouses. Then in the chapter on Lighting Chancel Drama, I suggested a licensed electrician for a church hookup. However, between these two situations there is a considerable "gray" area — the small civic clubs and such where small touring companies, usually by van or station wagon, are engaged for cultural programs. Invariably, these companies carry a collection of dimmers for "milking" individual outlets but often they also have a multiple receptacle box for a central hookup where possible in order to "speed things up." A homemade box is shown. The leads can be attached to the "starred" points on the circuit panel in the diagram at the beginning of this section.

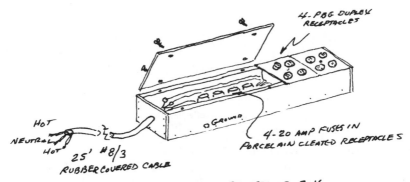

4 - PBG DUPLEX
RECEPTACLES

HOT
NEUTRAL
HOT
25' #8/3
RUBBER COVERED CABLE

GROUND

4-20 AMP FUSES IN
PORCELAIN CLEATED RECEPTACLES

MULTIPLE RECEPTACLE BOX
FOR CENTRAL HOOKUP

Riser Diagrams

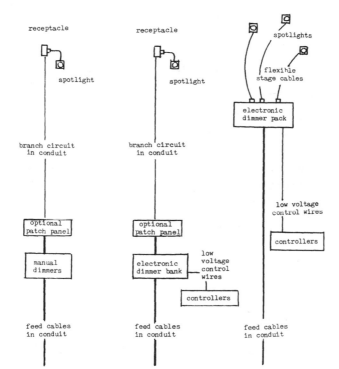

receptacle

spotlight

branch circuit
in conduit

optional
patch panel

manual
dimmers

feed cables
in conduit

receptacle

spotlight

branch circuit
in conduit

optional
patch panel

electronic
dimmer bank

low
voltage
control
wires

controllers

feed cables
in conduit

spotlights

flexible
stage cables

electronic
dimmer pack

low voltage
control wires

controllers

feed cables
in conduit

Riser diagrams are the means by which engineers chart the flow of such items as electricity, water, heating and air conditioning within a building or project. They are distinct from plans in that they conceptualize the actions involved. Shown on page 75 are three ways by which electrical current is controlled and brought to spotlights.

At left and center are the usual methods by which current is distributed to spotlights and other specialized fixtures within a theatre building. An interconnecting or "patch" panel permits the grouping of selected branch circuits with specific dimmers, often simplifying control. These riser diagrams also indicate that a patch panel need not be an integral part of a dimmer bank, though it usually is in order to keep large capacity wire runs to a minimum. With the manual system on the left, the operator must be stationed at the dimmer bank. With electronic dimmers, the operator can be located anywhere desired. The riser diagram on the right shows a system wherein the central dimmer bank, a patch panel, and permanently installed branch circuits are eliminated, in favor of a series of separate dimmer packs located in the general vicinity of the lights they will serve. This solution involves extension cables of various lengths and thus encourages a little more flexibility in the placing of the spotlights.

Of course, these diagrams are symbolic and simplistic. But they will give us a basis for further discussion. Note that with electronic dimmers the controllers can be located anywhere since the cost of the low voltage control wires is inconsequential and no conduit is required. In certain situations, as on catwalks, etc., dimmer packs can be located adjacent to their loads and branch circuits eliminated. Eventually the industry will work to a dimmer per light and "patching" will take place with the controllers only.

Though some riser diagrams may contain a great deal of additional information such as loads, wire sizes and even equipment types, it must be remembered that riser diagrams are not substitutes for the electrical engineering sheets which show the circuitry overlaid on the actual building plans. However, a good riser diagram simplifies the reading of these sheets, as anyone will agree who has pored over a typical electrical plan and that considerable maze of wiring.

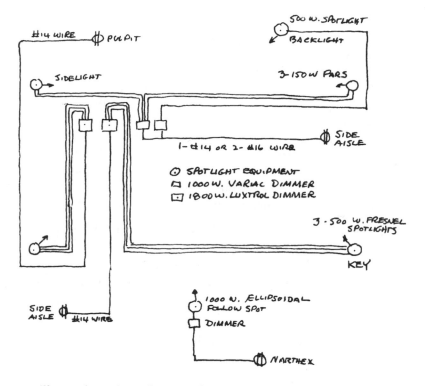

Shown is a riser diagram for assembling portable equipment for a production in a cathedral-style church. In this particular church there are eight separately fused outlets within the sanctuary. Dimmers (1) and (2) are 1800-watt Luxtrol autotransformer units in homemade containers as shown elsewhere. I have three output receptacles to each dimmer and one additional receptacle bypassing the dimmer so that I can keep one spot with a "cool" filter running along with low-key church illumination and the two other spots with "warm" filters reading for overlighting on cue. The remaining dimmers were Variacs, 1000-watt, an autotransformer dimmer now made for laboratory work by *Genrad*. One troublesome feature of this power solution is the amount of cable involved. Electronic dimmers with controllers would eliminate most of it.

Connectors

The term "receptacle" on the riser diagrams brings up the subject of connectors, a complex one. In domestic wiring one is familiar with the parallel blade or Edison plug and its corresponding receptacle. Ordinarily, these plugs are reversible, but sometimes they are not, one blade being slightly wider than the other. The latter has to do with sorting out the "neutral" side of the wiring from the "hot" side as explained in *The Nature of Power Hookups*. This has something to do with sound systems. Ordinarily, it does not matter which way the plug goes in.

The common household parallel blade plug is technically rated for 15 amps. Convenience receptacles are generally duplex, and their wiring is usually fused at 20 amps. So you could tap this receptacle for two 1000-watt spotlights on separate extension cords.

There is a heavier duty parallel blade plug and receptacle rated at 20 amps that takes the 15-amp plug as well and it is this plug and connector that I like to use in my theatres for reasons of flexibility in connecting a wide range of equipment. And if you are putting together a theatre through remodeling you can have the electrician wire the locations you desire in the usual manner of domestic wiring.

In larger theatres, especially those with working lofts, the situation is quite different. With the road show, where an entire lighting system is brought along, flexible cables run from the dimmer board directly to the lights wherever they may be. So you have bundles of cables of various lengths tied or taped together, some tied to pipe battens. All in all, cabling a road show is a considerable operation and one with which I was most familiar in the early years.

In a typical civic auditorium a certain amount of equipment is permanently installed for general purpose use. Where rigging is involved receptacles are mounted in "plugging strips," long metal channels containing the circuit wiring. These strips are fed from multi-wire cables which drop from the grid. Other circuits are wired to receptacles in boxes sunk into the stage floor to the sides and rear, boxes that are often called "pockets" or "dips." Circuits to beam positions in the ceiling of the auditorium are wired in the conventional way.

It is obvious that "plugging strips" have a specialized use, but they keep showing up on projects where they are not needed and often in the way, especially on catwalks (other than rigged, moving catwalks), obstructing valuable mounting space.

The favorite connector and receptacle in the professional theatre is a 20-amp pin connector, with ¼" diameter pins and sleeves. It is made of fiber and is virtually indestructible. It is flat and not as dangerous underfoot as a round plug. Unfortunately, this connector is not widely used outside the theatre trade. As a result, twistlock connectors often show up, and these are not as serviceable or useful.

Some years ago a safety feature was added to connectors and receptacles, a grounding system (presumably so that current from a loose wire in a piece of equipment cannot shortcut through a worker) and this third wire complicated connectors. The blades and pins remained the same — new pins were added. The old plugs still fit in the new receptacles but new plugs don't fit in the old receptacles. So all sorts of adapters are made up. This also means that there are three wires to connect instead of two. Generally speaking, with the two wires it didn't really matter which wire went to which terminal but the grounding wire has to be right. So between the new system and all the adapters many mistakes are made continually, resulting in dead shorts.

When ordering stage lighting equipment from a manufacturer one can usually specify the type of connector desired. For the boondocks I recommend staying with the parallel-blade or Edison connector. But if your equipment is being interchanged with other theatres check out the type of connecting system used and decide which way to go — adaptive or compatible.

CHAPTER 10

Reading Catalogs and "Spec" Sheets

Collecting catalogs and equipment performance sheets is an important part of the young technician's education, and the best place to do this is at theatre conferences where there are commercial exhibit areas. Here one can both see a goodly amount of equipment and talk with manufacturers' representatives as well. However, if one reads the trade magazines such as *Theatre Crafts* and *Lighting Dimensions*, such material can also be assembled by mail.

Promotional material is published in three ways: by general catalogs from "scenic" houses which list a wide range of theatrical equipment and supplies; by equipment specialty folders, usually an 8½" x 11" sheet folded once (for example, a folder listing a variety of ellipsoidal spotlights by a particular company); and by single sheets, which describe particular pieces of lighting equipment in detail on one side, with performance specifications on the other, such as spreads, brilliance and brightness at stated distances. Lighting companies used to issue general catalogs but more recently have favored the single data sheets, since customized loose-leaf folders can be made up for a variety of specific situations. Among the older general lighting catalogs, the best known perhaps was the *Century Lighting* catalog of the 1940s, often used as a supplementary text in schools and colleges.

However, starting out with single data sheets can be a confusing experience for the young technician unless he has studied the field of lighting and read some textbooks. It is better that he find a general catalog which describes the functions of the different types of lighting equipment and which indicates the more useful models. From this vantage point he will then be able to analyze the single data sheets more intelligently.

Let's suppose that we are looking for an ellipsoidal reflector spotlight for a moderately sized stage. Right off we may be in trouble, for someone might say, "You mean a 'leko,' don't you?" Well, yes and no. Actually, "leko" is an acronym for an ellipsoidal spotlight manufactured by the old Century Lighting Co., but like the term "gel" as applied to any type of color filter, it has crept into backstage lingo. So if we find a data sheet issued by the Strand Century Co. we will find a "leko," while in a Kliegl or Hub catalog this type will be an "ellipsoidal" spotlight.

One of the best catalogs for theatrical supplies is that of the Olesen Co., 1535 Ivar Ave., Hollywood, CA 90028. Turning to the section on Stage Lights we find an introduction to spotlights in general, and the ellipsoidal reflector or Fresnel types distinguished in particular. Under Catalog No. 10357 we read: "The most popular and versatile of the Ellipsoidal Spot Lights…This unit will produce a circle of light approximately 14' in diameter at a distance of 20'." Further, we notice that two 6" x 9" plano-convex lenses are involved, and that the spotlight will take either 500- or 700-watt lamps.

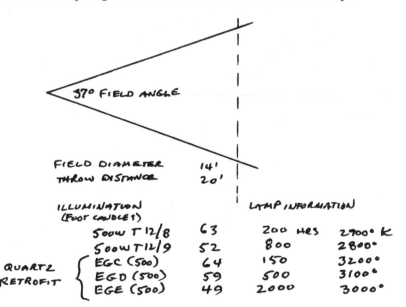

At this point one should turn to an individual data sheet for more details. So I checked another manufacturer's data sheet for an ellipsoidal spotlight of a similar spread and lens configuration, as shown above. A number of different lamps are listed, several of which are "quartz" retrofits. For an explanation of this, see the following section on Lamps. Obviously, a practical choice involves either the 500T12/9 or the EGD. The quartz will be the more expensive and the color temperature is closer to the television ideal of 3200°, but for live audiences only the 500WT12/9 with its color temperature of 2800° will be perfectly satisfactory.

However, on a preceding page of the Olesen catalog there is another ellipsoidal spotlight with the same lens system, but one which will accept only a quartz lamp. Upon further examination one notes that the lamps in these two models are mounted differently. With the latter model the lamp is mounted "axially," that is, thrust into the reflector through the center, whereas with the other model the lamp comes through the reflector from the side. If we search out a comparative data sheet on this we find that the axially mounted lamp is the more efficient one, and that we pick up at least another 10 foot candles.

One should assume that the published foot candle readings are the best that can be obtained, and are taken at the dead center of the beam. But two spreads are given, the "beam" and the "field." These angles, in this case 24° and 37° respectively, have to do with a fall-off in brilliance from the center portion of the spotlight beam to the outer edge. The beam angle is established at that diameter where the fall-off does not exceed 50% of the beam center reading, while the field angle extends to 10% of the center reading. This means that the "circle of light" described in general terms is perhaps overly optimistic.

It should also be assumed that the published foot candle readings are taken when the beam is "peaked" rather than "flatted." A peak field is one where the lamp and reflector are adjusted to produce the brightest possible beam center. A flat field is one where the overall field is even, though it may be somewhat dimmer. With the older incandescent type ellipsoidals this adjustment is time consuming. With the newer, axially mounted lamps, the adjustment is simpler, so this option is mentioned more often.

In our merry chase we have pursued only one particular ellipsoidal reflector spotlight, the "workhorse," as it is described, but all around are others with narrower or wider beam spreads. The narrower ones are used chiefly for longer throws such as in outdoor theatres, or from auditorium ceilings in proscenium theatres, while the wider ones are used for sidelighting for dance or for very small stages.

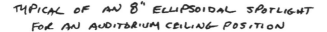

TYPICAL OF AN 8" ELLIPSOIDAL SPOTLIGHT FOR AN AUDITORIUM CEILING POSITION

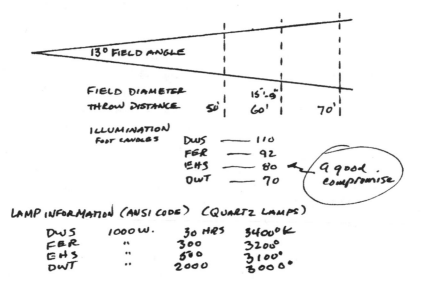

Above is a typical spotlight data sheet for an auditorium ceiling position. For a throw of 60' from a large civic auditorium ceiling and taking into consideration the circular field and overlapping, I would recommend 12 of the spotlights, 6 from each direction for complete crosslighting, using Roscolux Bastard Amber 02 and Surprise Pink 51 color filters. On the other hand, to "soup up" an existing set of lights, I would recommend 6 units set straight on with No Color Straw 06 or Pale Yellow 07.

Of late, however, there are models which have variable beams, a flexibility that has been difficult to achieve with this type of spotlight in a moderate price range. These newer spots can be divided into two groups: those with manually interchangeable lenses which fit into prearranged slots; and those whose variability of beam width is achieved by adjusting moveable lenses, in much the same way as the large follow spotlights operate.

The ellipsoidal spotlight was also chosen as an example for two additional reasons: currently it is a highly competitive product, with a great deal of up-to-date engineering applied to it; and because, with the new Rosco diffusion filters an ellipsoidal can substitute for a Fresnel spotlight, and while this is a costly substitution, the flexibility might be attractive enough to compensate.

Lamps

Most catalogs have a page or two showing drawings of the various lamp types. As with lenses, the suitable lamps are specified along with the lighting equipment. Unlike lenses, however, there are several options within a lamp type with the choice left up to the user. These options include color temperature ratings, lamp life in hours, and, in some cases, a choice between a tungsten incandescent or tungsten-halogen (quartz) lamps. Lamp charts also show the foot candles, or brilliance, at various distances from the spotlight, and depending upon the lamp type.

Color temperature has to do with the "whiteness" of light. Color temperature is critical with film emulsions and television cameras. The ideal for most camera situations is 3200° Kelvin. However, this is not necessary for live audiences. In fact, many lighting artists prefer a warmer or softer illumination. You will notice that as the "whiteness" is reduced somewhat the lamp life in hours usually increases.

One of the more recent developments in stage lighting has been the introduction of the tungsten halogen lamp, often called a "quartz" lamp. Unlike the older tungsten incandescent lamps, these newer lamps contain chemicals which reduce the blackening of the envelope. This is very important for television and motion pictures, and it was primarily for these media that the quartz lamps were developed. Unfortunately, for this chemical cycle to work the lamps must burn at a higher temperature, hence the quartz instead of glass for the envelope. And a higher burning temperature means more heat-resistant color filters, at increased prices, of course. Also, great care must be taken in handling these lamps, for if any grease, even from the fingers, touches the quartz a burnout will occur in short order.

Many quartz lamps can be obtained with two types of bases, one which permits the lamp to be substituted for the older tungsten incandescent lamps, and one which fits only the newer equipment. The former are called "retrofits." I don't see much sense in making this substitution though. If you wish to use quartz lamps in spotlights, then purchase the newer equipment, in which the lamp is axially mounted, and is easily adjustable. First, a better field of light results, and second, the ease of adjustment makes it possible to go from a field of light with a brilliant center to one that is "flatted," that is, a somewhat less brilliant but overall a more even field.

One should also avoid the use of quartz lamps in scoops. There is no substitute for the old tungsten pear-shaped, inside frost mogul screw base lamps for an even field of diffuse illumination.

CHAPTER 11

Homemade Equipment

For those working on tight budgets there is a considerable amount of equipment which can be made up in the basement hobby shop. And one of the first questions I am asked concerns those little electronic wall dimmers you can pick up at the hardware store for chandeliers and such. These will work — but there are two things you should know. They are not static-free as anyone with a remote phone will know only too well. Also, they cannot be "hot patched," that is, the load cannot be connected after one has been turned on. The directions so state — and this is why they are used for permanently connected fixtures such as chandeliers. So if you are careful and don't have a problem with a sound system, they are okay.

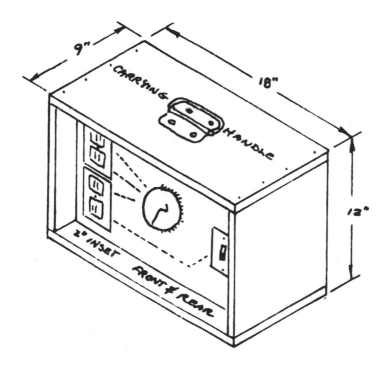

My own preference runs to autotransformers, although these are becoming increasingly difficult to obtain. Shown on the previous page is a standard Superior Electric Co. Luxtrol 1800-watt wall box dimmer housed in a case of my own manufacture.

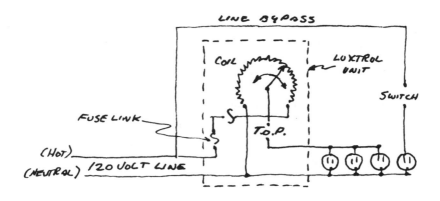

The box is made up of ¾" pine wood. The "face plate" is a panel of ½" plywood as is the rear panel. These panels are inset for security in traveling and are screwed to ¾" x 4" strips fastened to the inner sides of the box. A large wooden cleat is fastened to the rear panel and around this a feed cord can be wound. A wiring diagram is shown.

One may very well wonder how to tell which way a parallel-blade type plug for the feed is to be inserted into a wall receptacle when there is no ground pin. For a single dimmer such as we have shown, or a number of smaller capacity dimmers not over a 15- or 20-amp circuit service, it doesn't matter. What does matter is getting the internal wiring down correctly as shown. With larger dimmer packages requiring higher capacity feed cables connected directly to electrical distribution panels, the cables must always be identified as hot(s) and neutral. See the section on Power Hookups. This dimmer could control the spotlights mounted on the homemade stand shown on the next page.

A Spotlight Stand

The popular 6" 500-watt Fresnel spotlight produces just such a "splash" — a directional soft-edged beam of light whose spread is variable by moving the lamp back and forth within the reflector housing. Here the spotlights are mounted on a homemade stand. The spotlight will include the color frame and a C-clamp suitable for pipe mounting, but not the lamp or electrical connector. You don't need the C-clamp and I'm told it costs more to unpack the box to remove it than the clamp is worth. A 6" Fresnel spotlight costs about $60 and the lamp about $50.

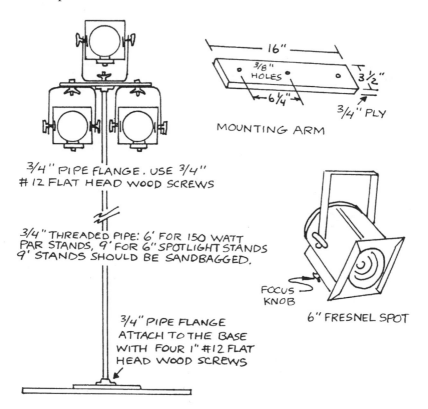

16"

3/8" HOLES

3 1/2"

6 1/4"

3/4" PLY

MOUNTING ARM

3/4" PIPE FLANGE. USE 3/4" #12 FLAT HEAD WOOD SCREWS

3/4" THREADED PIPE: 6' FOR 150 WATT PAR STANDS, 9' FOR 6" SPOTLIGHT STANDS 9' STANDS SHOULD BE SANDBAGGED.

3/4" PIPE FLANGE ATTACH TO THE BASE WITH FOUR 1" #12 FLAT HEAD WOOD SCREWS

FOCUS KNOB

6" FRESNEL SPOT

Before attaching the pipe flange to the adapter with four ¾" #12 screws, insert a ⅜" bolt at center, placing a piece of cardboard over the bolt head and between the flange and adapter to prevent the bolt from falling down into the pipe and to keep the bolt firm when the nut is tightened. Use 1½" bolts for metal spotlight yokes and 2½" bolts for the homemade PAR yokes.

Bases of ¾" ply: 2½' minimum diameter for 6" spotlights as shown; 2' diameter for lower stands for 150-watt PAR units or follow spot. Build up base with ¾" ply disc 1' in diameter and screw to base with four to six 1½ #9 flat head wood screws.

I also use the same dimmer for a follow spot unit I made up with a 1000-watt standard ellipsoidal. The operating height may be adjusted by changing the 26" pipe for one of a different length.

Follow Spot and Stand

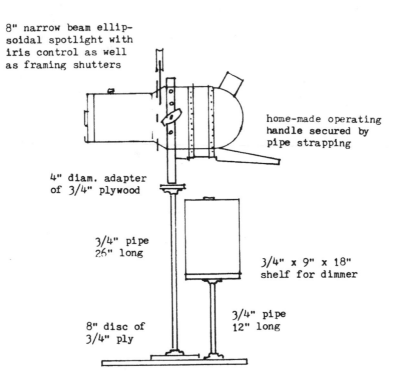

8" narrow beam ellip-
soidal spotlight with
iris control as well
as framing shutters

home-made operating
handle secured by
pipe strapping

4" diam. adapter
of 3/4" plywood

3/4" pipe
26" long

3/4" x 9" x 18"
shelf for dimmer

3/4" pipe
12" long

8" disc of
3/4" ply

2' diam. base
of 3/4" plywood

The PAR Revolution

The next step up in economy is the professional PAR can. PARs are lensless instruments which take rugged sealed beam reflector lamps in a variety of sizes, shapes and wattages. The smallest take the 150- to 300-watt PAR lamps, and these are the ones recommended for our use. Don't underrate these simple instruments — the PAR 64s, from 500 to 1000 watts, are the backbone of "rock concert" lighting. The can resembles a Fresnel spotlight without the adjustable lamp base. The 150- to 300-watt cans cost about $35, the 150-watt lamp, easily available from hardware stores and building supply centers, cost under $10, the 300 watt, not always a local shelf item, is slightly more.

What you have in PARs is a rough sort of spotlight — not as fuzzy as a Fresnel and not as defined as an ellipsoidal. However, with the PAR 38 we have a lamp that is available at any hardware store and its medium screw base will fit in a standard cleated socket. Shown on the following page is a useful stand and PAR 38 units, plus snap-on gel frame holder snoots from the Olesen Co., 1535 Ivar Ave., Hollywood, CA 90028. The PAR lamp plus the Olesen Snoot will balance perfectly in the yoke if the dimensions shown are followed carefully.

The PAR 38 can take a lamp with a medium screw base. At this point we move into homemade lighting fixtures, for a medium screw base is readily available in many lamp holder devices sold right off the hardware store and building supply center shelves. Cleated sockets are also found in most hardware stores. With these, plus some large vegetable cans, a variety of floodlights can be fashioned that are only limited by your imagination. The down side will be the attachment of color frames of some sort for most of these solutions, for color media (commonly and perhaps erroneously called "gels") must not contact the lamps. They are also flexible enough to require some sort of frame.

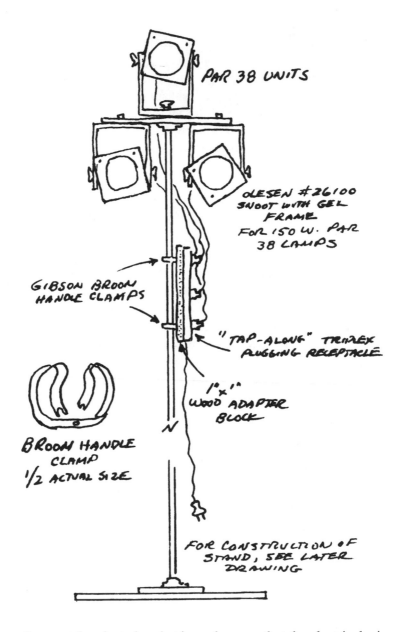

PAR 38 UNITS

OLESEN #26100 SNOOT WITH GEL FRAME FOR 150 W. PAR 38 LAMPS

GIBSON BROOM HANDLE CLAMPS

"TAP-ALONG" TRIPLEX PLUGGING RECEPTACLE

1" x 1" WOOD ADAPTER BLOCK

BROOM HANDLE CLAMP 1/2 ACTUAL SIZE

FOR CONSTRUCTION OF STAND, SEE LATER DRAWING

I mount the cleated socket in such a way that the electrical wire entering the unit does not touch any metal, a safety precaution. This construction is a little involved and is described on page 93.

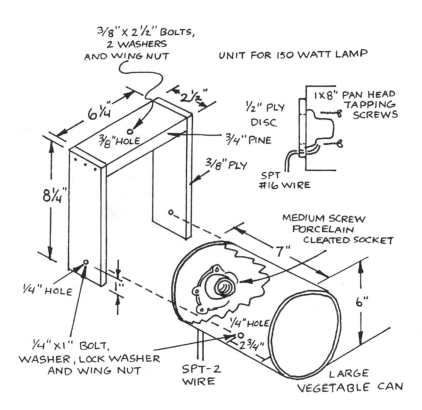

3/8" x 2½" BOLTS, 2 WASHERS AND WING NUT

UNIT FOR 150 WATT LAMP

6¼"

2½"

½" PLY DISC

3/4" PINE

3/8" HOLE

3/8" PLY

1x8" PAN HEAD TAPPING SCREWS

SPT #16 WIRE

8¼"

¼" HOLE

1"

¼" x 1" BOLT, WASHER, LOCK WASHER AND WING NUT

MEDIUM SCREW PORCELAIN CLEATED SOCKET

7"

6"

¼" HOLE

2¾"

SPT-2 WIRE

LARGE VEGETABLE CAN

This sectional drawing shows the bottom of the can, a cleated socket, a 4" diameter disc of ½" ply and the electrical cord. For assembly, place the can, open end down, on the work table. Center the disc on the back of the can, then the cleated socket on top of the disc. *Hold firmly* while drilling three holes with a ⅛" bit, two

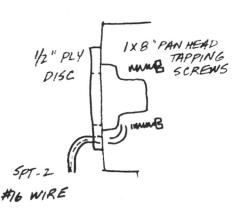

½" PLY DISC

1x8" PAN HEAD TAPPING SCREWS

SPT-2 #16 WIRE

through the socket's cleat holes and one about half an inch away from the socket. These holes should be drilled all the way through the bottom of the can.

Remove socket and disc. The ⅛" holes that are aligned with the cleated socket will later serve as feeler holes for the 1" #8 pan head tapping screws. Enlarge these holes in the can bottom to ¹¹⁄₆₄". Enlarge the third disc hole to ⁵⁄₁₆" and enlarge the matching hole in the can bottom to ⅜". Cut a length of #16 SPT-2 wire, pull through the disc (it will fit quite snugly) and then insert it through the hole in the can. Secure the electrical wire to the terminals of the cleated socket. Now align the plywood disc, the socket and the holes in the can, and secure with the tapping screws. By this operation, not only is the socket mounted firmly but the wire is prevented from coming into contact with the metal can bottom as it passes through.

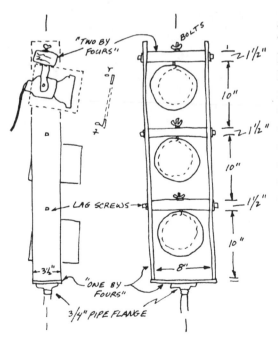

Shown at left is a unit made with "weatherproof lampholders" from local hardware stores. Remove both ends of 6" diameter vegetable cans and drill holes one inch from the ends. The lampholder and can are secured to the 2 x 4 by a bolt and wing nut. A disc with center removed is secured to seat taped on gels. Use with 150-watt PAR 38s. This is an excellent unit for sidelighting.

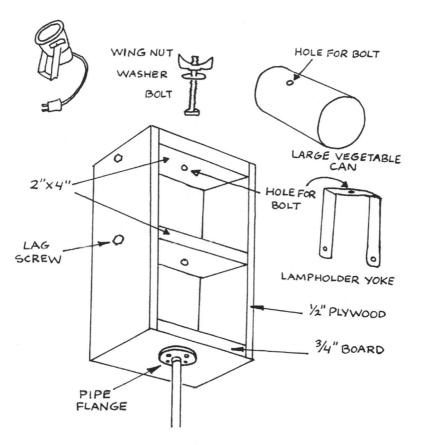

WING NUT
WASHER
BOLT

HOLE FOR BOLT

LARGE VEGETABLE CAN

2"x4"

HOLE FOR BOLT

LAG SCREW

LAMPHOLDER YOKE

½" PLYWOOD

¾" BOARD

PIPE FLANGE

A sturdier and even more economical unit that starts with a lampholder from the hardware store or building supply center is shown upper left. The ones I used came with a base plate to fit a standard electrical box plus an L-shaped ground stake. You need only the yoke and socket. Then remove both top and bottom from a large 6" vegetable can found at a nearby restaurant trash barrel. Slip a bolt through the yoke (you will have to temporarily remove the socket), then up through a hole in the can, then through a hole in the 2 x 4. The 2 x 4 is lag-screwed into the one-half inch plywood sides of the unit so that it can be tilted since you may not have enough play in the yoke for upward or downward adjustment. Bolting some small angle irons to the can will secure a color frame. Spray all parts flat black.

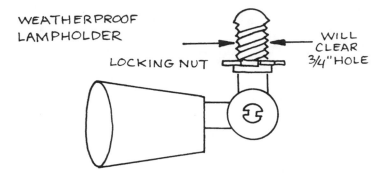

WEATHERPROOF
LAMPHOLDER

LOCKING NUT

WILL
CLEAR
¾"HOLE

In this ever-changing world, the last time I checked my hardware and building supply stores I could not find the yoked lampholder but found plenty of these security light brackets which screw into dual outlet boxes for placement under the eaves of homes. I was able to purchase the single piece shown for considerably less than the yoked bracket. By notching the 2 x 4 and nailing a piece of ⅜" or ¼" ply across the notch this bracket can be secured through a ¾" hole by means of the locking washer.

I like to make up these vertical strip units with three to four lamps, although taller strips may be necessary to build up a sufficient volume of light. This is something we haven't discussed — but the whole subject of brilliance is so relative that adding up foot candles is unnecessary. A rule of thumb may be useful: if you double the number of lights aimed at a particular target you will get half as much again of that brilliance. Adding a third light will give you a fourth as much again. For example: if your initial reading is 20 foot candles, aiming a second light will raise the reading to about 30, and the third light to a total of 35. This is called "the waterfall" principle by illuminating engineers.

Another inexpensive method of mounting lamp receptacles is "track lighting," where adjustable lampholders clamp onto metal sleeves complete with inbuilt circuits. I find these assemblies most useful for floor-based mounting behind ground rows. Track lighting parts are found in home building supply centers along with 50-watt R-40 medium screw base lamps, although a wide variety of other lamps can be used for low level illumination.

A Backing Striplight

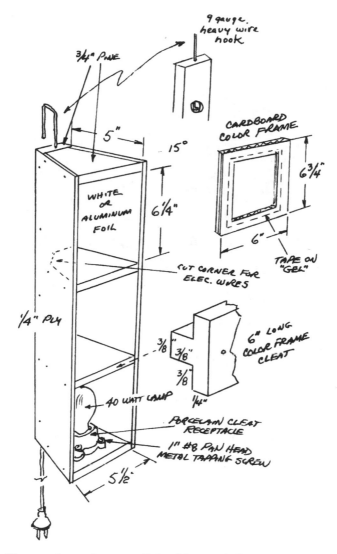

Shown above is a small backing striplight. Usually made of metal and painted aluminum or white gloss inside, and using four or more lamps from 25 to 100 watts, these open striplights were standard equipment during the heyday of "box" sets, but have since disappeared from the marketplace.

    Shown below is an enlarged view of the sidelighting system described in the section on Civic Theatres. It can easily be constructed using the Olesen 29170 tee.

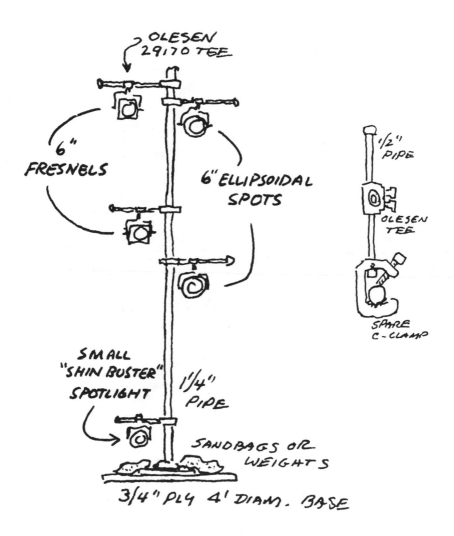

A most useful lighting prop for church plays is a hand-carried lantern.

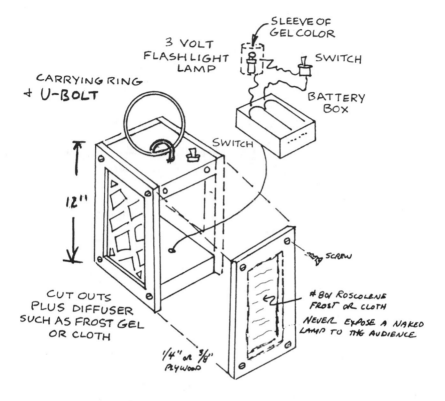

Start with two 9" squares of ¾" soft pine to form the base and top. From Upsonite or other lightweight panel board cut the face plates as follows: two 9" x 12" and two 9+" x 12" as shown. Secure either thin white cloth or diffusion "gels" to the rear. Three of these panels can be secured permanently and will form the structure of the lantern. The fourth should be removable to service the lamp and batteries.

Build a little box to contain the two flashlight batteries in such a way that you can jam the batteries against the metal contact strips which you have fashioned from tin can stock. Wire the batteries in series. Solder wires to a three-volt flashlight lamp and intercept the circuit with a switch. A small sleeve or cylinder of plastic "gel" around the lamp will provide the color.

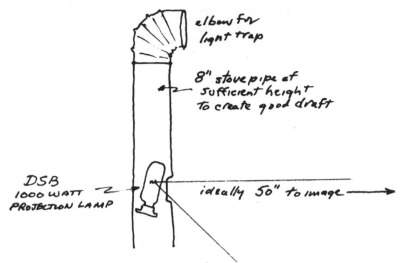

elbow for
light trap

8" stovepipe of
sufficient height
to create good draft

DSB
1000 WATT
PROJECTION LAMP

ideally 50" to image ⟶

MILLER LAMPHOUSE

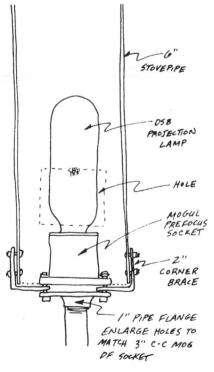

6"
STOVEPIPE

DSB
PROJECTION
LAMP

HOLE

MOGUL
PREFOCUS
SOCKET

2"
CORNER
BRACE

1" PIPE FLANGE
ENLARGE HOLES TO
MATCH 3" C-C MOG
PF SOCKET

At right is a simplified working diagram of my "stovepipe lamphouse" for the Colored Shadow Projection System described in the following section. The drawing shows the projection lamp tipped forward. The angle should not exceed 10°. This not only improves the intensity, aligning the axis of the filament closer to the angle of throw, but also reduces "ghost" images which result from light reflection from the glass of the lamp envelope directly behind the filament.

I find a stovepipe very useful. The higher the stovepipe the better the air flow, and projection lamps get very hot.

Top off the stovepipe with an elbow for a nice light trap. Partial stovepipe lengths not snapped together can be used to trim the hole for the path of the light.

Lamps and Sockets

The particular lamp is not important save that it be as much a point source of light as possible which means that it should be a squarish filament. I have used the projection line 500-watt CZX/DAB and the 750-watt DDB, both medium prefocus, and the 1000-watt DSB, with mogul prefocus base. The DSB filament is approximately ½" wide, which means that the image should be 50" away, about as far as you can conveniently go. All these filaments are "biplane," which means that the filament is in two parts, one part behind the other and offset for maximum compaction. With all the new lamps on the market, there are probably many others which will serve as well. Sockets can be had from manufacturers. It goes without saying that the lamp must be rigidly mounted — the slightest movement will be multiplied ten times over and make the audience seasick.

CHAPTER 12

Projected Scenery

There has been no development in scenography as controversial as that of projected scenery. But first I would like to point out that I truly believe there is an important difference between projected *backgrounds*, especially my own system as described in the following section, and projected *scenery*, that is, the substitution of projections for scenery in the immediate vicinity of the actors. Again, we are dealing with art forms, and given changing times and circumstances, history has demonstrated again and again that eventually "anything goes."

When projections were first introduced into the theatre they were considered to be replacements for painted backdrops and such. And lens equipment was considered essential for that sort of detail. The problem was getting equipment which would provide an image of sufficient width at a reasonable throw distance. Then came an art form known as Multimedia and "projections" took on new meanings. Even home slide projectors and overhead classroom projectors got into the act. Then this art form became kinetic, and a whole new line of effect equipment came into being, or perhaps "into motion." (See Patterns, following.) Rear projections became more practical with the development of a new translucent material called Roscoscreen, by Rosco. Furthermore, this new material could be slit vertically, allowing actors (and even furniture) to move through the imagery. Then came holography, and the apparent suspension of three-dimensional imagery in space, used with such stunning effect in Disneyland's "Haunted House."

However, the main purpose of this book is to "bring light to bear," primarily upon the actor and the scenery and props in a reasonable and inexpensive manner. "Effects" as such really lie beyond this basic subject matter. The important thing to realize, though, is that all of these contemporary effects, to some degree, are within reach of the amateur's pocketbook, with the payoff through artful use rather than by means of sophisticated equipment.

Patterns

With the ellipsoidal spotlight one has a projection system of sorts, for metal patterns that are inserted in the shutter plane will appear reasonably clear on background surfaces. Television was early on in the use of abstract patterns to give texture to backgrounds for talk shows. These first patterns were made from pieces of machinery guards or perforated pie tins. More recently the development of stainless steel patterns by photochemical etching has advanced this art to a highly sophisticated level. Write the Olesen Co. for their Special Effects Lighting Equipment folder. Also the Great American Market, P.O. Box 178, Woodland Hills, CA 91364. It is recommended that pattern slots be specified for all ellipsoidal spotlights other than those with iris control.

Lensless Projections

Projections in the theatre are controversial only when thought of as substitutes for realistic scenery with which an actor is directly involved. Otherwise they can be most useful, especially in enlarging the idea of an environment already expressed. A projection can be as simple as an etched steel pattern slipped into the slot of an ellipsoidal spotlight or as sophisticated as a photographic image rear-projected upon a translucent backdrop vertically slit for an actor's pass-through. The technology is in place and well advertised.

Other than ellipsoidal pattern projections there are problems with lens projections which limit their appeal to the harried technicians working in the boondocks: the equipment is expensive; distortion must be corrected in one way or another; and the preparation of an image (or slide) can be time-consuming. Some form of shadow projection is far more practical. The only challenge is: how sophisticated can this sort of imagery be? The answer is: far more than one would imagine if he only has in mind the old Linnebach lantern.

When Linnebach is mentioned, what most readily comes to mind are those rather fuzzy backgrounds of silhouettes or color transparencies usually associated with the moody skies and abstract mountains of Appia's sets for Wagnerian operas. But the Linnebach lantern is still in use today and its appeal over the years has been its simplicity, low cost and wide coverage, exceeding that of any single lens system. A typical lantern is shown below, of a design suitable for a cyclorama projection from a floor position concealed by platforms or groundrows.

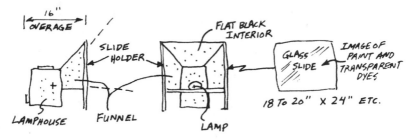

The only parts absolutely essential to a lensless projection are the lamp filament and the slide. The lantern housing masks unwanted light and provides a place to mount the socket and hold the slide. Since only the light from the lamp filament is desired the interior is painted flat black to avoid reflection. As to the lamp, the smaller the filament the better, though brightness is a factor. For many years a favorite was the 1000-watt G-type lamp with either a mogul screw or prefocus base.

In the late 1940s I met a fellow who had some ideas for improving the Linnebach lantern. His name was Thomas Wilfred. He did three very important things: he used a smaller filament, he distanced the lamp from the slide, and he separated the slide from the lamp housing. With these improvements the clarity of the projection was enhanced, the slide no longer had a heat problem,

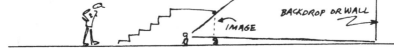

and the slide, now free of the lamphouse, could be kept parallel to the projection surface thus eliminating "keystoning" or distortion. Of course, Wilfred no longer had a single piece of equipment. Instead, he had an arrangement of parts in space!

First, let's take these three improvements as an arrangement in space and apply them to an image projected onto a backdrop or back wall from beneath a masking platform.The lamp socket is screwed to the floor.

The image can be as simple as a potted plant or as complex as elaborate cutouts with gels taped over the openings. Or transparent dyes on clear acetate. Where silhouettes are involved flanking flood-lights color the shadow areas.

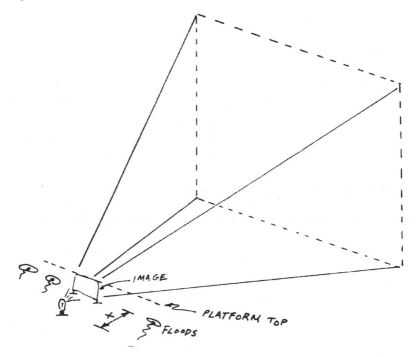

But this is only the beginning of the wonders of Wilfred's pro-jection world. Since the distance of the slide from the lamp filament is variable the slide can be broken into planes with some elements of an image closer to the lamp and others farther away, resulting in varying degrees of clarity. For example, in *South Pacific*, palm trees along the beach should appear clear while the distant island Bali Ha'i would look better if hazy.

Wilfred also realized that time-of-day segues are important. For this he invented an ingenious "mood" changer consisting of slowly moving, overlapping frames containing arrangeable strips of colored glass placed as close as possible to the lamp filament. As for moving cloud "diorama" effects Wilfred concocted a giant revolving acetate drum around the housing for his lamp.

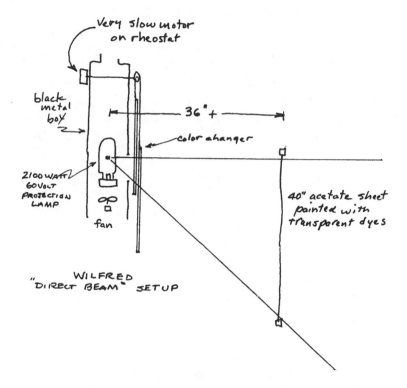

The Wilfred color changer consisted of two frames into which narrow strips of clear glass can be inserted. The frames are suspended by a single string which passes over a pulley wheel that can be made to turn *very slowly* at will. Thus one frame will descend and the other frame ascend simultaneously before the aperture of the lamphouse. By coating the glass strips with various tints of transparent dyes, the "time of day" of a projection can be subtly altered. The proximity of these strips to the light source and the resultant lack of resolution camouflages the means by which the effects are achieved.

The only remaining problem for Wilfred was where to put his

arrangement of parts other than under concealing platforms — and now rather high platforms at that. He solved the problem by going overhead, initially above the first teaser position. In this he had the help of the artistic director at the University of Washington in Seattle, John Ashby Conway. Professor Conway was at the time in charge of four playhouses each with a rotating production schedule, a position which incurred both heavy responsibilities and great possibilities — even to the point of selecting appropriate performance styles. I mention this because it is of tremendous importance to the birth of new ideas. The other ambience in which new ideas are easily born is poverty, of having to do without accustomed benefits and being willing to try anything to get ahead. Fortunately, this is the ambience of the boondocks and it is why I am able to write this book!

Following is a description of how the projection images were made for the Baylor University Centennial production of *Towers on the Brazos*. The images had to do with buildings and other familiar campus scenes as backdrops to the dramatic action on the stage and on the flanking platforms:

After the acetate is attached to the frame a preliminary sketch is placed underneath. Since the solvent in the dye reacts with the acetate a smooth coloring is virtually impossible and the painting will have an inbuilt "style." Short, broken strokes create a feeling of impressionism. Each brush stroke, when projected, will seem to have the brilliance of a piece of glass, with the color intensity greater on the outer edges of each stroke. Spaces between strokes give a lighter vitality to the final effect. Intermixing strokes of different colors also adds to color vitality. For dark, opaque lines, flat black latex must be applied thick enough to block out the passage of light. Such lines are best done first, and preferably on the obverse side. A clear space, almost ¼", must be left between the color and the black lines for line clarity in the projection. Dyes can be thinned and sprayed for a muted fog effect — but this will obliterate all detail.

Since colors will appear darker before the light transforms them, I found it necessary to test all color densities and mixes on a sheet of acetate prior to application, using the same lamp fila-

ment. This impressionist style of painting may appear mundane when observed by the naked eye, but lighting passing through the image has much the same effect as sun streaming through stained glass. For an absolutely clear color, apply gelatine or plastic color media with scotch tape, masked out by flat black latex. — Irene Corey

The image frames were 3½' by 5½', with 5 mil 40" acetate stretched over and secured by stapling through duct tape. Since cross-fading was desired the image frames were located side by side and two light sources were used. The 500-watt CZX projection lamp with a medium prefocus base was chosen. The image frames were 30" from the lamp filaments. This distance is arrived at by multiplying the lamp filament size by 100, in this instance, 100 (x) $\frac{5}{16}$" = 30". The degree of clarity obtained by this formula is such that a thread placed in the image position will be visible on the backdrop.

Image Size and Projection Span

In our discussion the reader may have noticed that the term "image" has been substituted for the term "slide." Actually, image may be the more accurate description, slide being associated with the old glass pane that slid into position across the face of the Linnebach black box. With the projection possibilities we are now talking about, an image may consist of many parts, so slide is hardly the word for it. But before we get into this we do need to know the maximum size of an image in a given theatre so that the catwalk framing can be designed.

You can expect a relatively even field width at least double the distance from the projection lamp filament to the projection surface at center. So the average image width will probably be around 8'. The height will be around 4'. The steepest angle of projection (from the lamp filament to the bottom of the backdrop) should not exceed 50°.

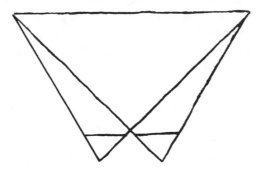

In the Baylor University production of *Towers on the Brazos,* the cross-fading imagery occupied about 12' of unobstructed width — no problem from the floor but something to be considered from above. To be on the safe side when framing up a catwalk for overhead projection I would leave 12' clear at the center. And there have been times when I have used a 12'-wide image from a single lamp though the brightness of an image 50'+ wide tends to fall off at the sides due to the inverse square law.

Eventually the magnificent space platform fell victim to the vicissitudes of time. Wilfred himself got no further with the system overhead because of the mounting problems when juxtaposed with working loft theatres. However, I had seen the system in its glory and I intended to develop it further.

There were, as I saw it, two requirements that had to be reckoned with if further developments were to take place. The first was that the ideal placement of the parts and the attendant masking precluded a proper working loft altogether and any installation should take place where no loft was contemplated. The second was that any scenery upstage of the projection platform would have to be so designed that the imagery could be projected over it! I also realized that only "in the boondocks" would one be able to satisfy these requirements for both run afoul of conventional stagecraft thinking. But in my own experience I had found the solutions — at least for myself.

Wilfred painted his imagery on clear acetate sheets with transparent dyes. The acetate stock he used was 40" which in turn accounts for the 36" distance between the lamp filament and the image. I desired to increase the clarity of the system so I placed the image farther away from the projection lamp filament, usually from 48" to 50". This required a larger image, usually 48" high, rather than the 40" clear acetate sheet. So I dispensed with the painting on acetate sheets and went to a more abstract type of imagery, more of a collage of perforated silhouettes with transparent colors such as gels taped on. Then I used scoops to color the dark areas. This revised system I named the colored Shadow Projection System.

Shown above is a sturdy catwalk which runs across the full width of the stage. The catwalk is surfaced on its underside and

takes the place of a conventional teaser. Upstage of the catwalk the space must be free and clear although additional masking can be placed above the image projection line. To either side of the image area spotlights and floodlights can be mounted. In addition to coloring backgrounds these floodlights play an important part in the fashioning of imagery and make Wilfred's "mood" changer unnecessary.

Up to this point in our discussion, the background projection has been conceived of in terms of illumination from one point source of light. The next step is to add floodlights flanking the image area from an overhead space platform, as shown in the previous illustration. This is easily done. I have found that for cycloramas up to 50' wide four 500-watt scoops, properly adjusted, will do nicely for each color wipe. Such an addition has opened up two new possibilities for the fashioning of projection imagery. If a giant tree limb were lashed across the image area we would have a magnificent silhouette projected, yet the shadows would be dark. By adding some dimmed scoops the shadows could be colored, yet the projected image would remain. On the other hand, some elaborate designs could be stenciled out of a large sheet of cardboard attached to the image frame and these designs projected upon a backdrop first colored by the scoops.

The remaining solution involved scenery of a sort over which the imagery could be projected. The inspiration for this came from the style of a store window display. When not out on tour it was my wont of an idle evening to stroll up Fifth Avenue and study the displays.

Unlike the typical theatrical setting which usually stretched from one side of the proscenium frame to the other, store window display involves "props" in a velvety iridescent sort of "nothingness" space beautifully lit.  Obviously, the answer to the problem of scenery with overhead projection lies in highly sophisticated *set pieces* rather than in complete sets — sets which grow out of an idea in space rather than sets which fill up the picture frame. There was nothing really new in set pieces — after all, I had been building such pieces for years for touring groups with limited transportation. But there is something new in placing such pieces in a different kind of atmosphere!

On proscenium stages one usually expects to see a scenic image that is "framed" in some fashion, ranging from the curved "sky" cyclorama all the way to a "box" set — a literal room interior with one wall removed. Of this type of imagery the proscenium frame is a vital part, suggesting that there is more of the same imagery, but just out of sight. Remove the frame and the illusion is gone.

On the other hand, the passerby who looks at a store window display rarely observes a "continuous" image of any sort beyond the very obvious frame. The frame serves only to define a neutral space. It is within this neutral space that the display is isolated.

Display men create these neutral or "nothingness" spaces with seamless felts adhered to smooth surfaces. The colors are in the darker shades of brown, gray or black. The lighting is selective and the sources discreetly located. The objects to be displayed are centered, away from backgrounds, and supporting props are kept to a minimum.

If the same principles are applied to a proscenium theatre, a fly loft is no longer required since the scenery will be freestanding, that is, contained entirely within the neutral space. This means that some sort of lighting grid or similar facility can be over the entire stage.

On the next page is a composite plan, showing the stage floor level to the left of the center line and the overhead catwalk plan to the right.

In this instance, a catwalk system is shown that is designed to service the majority of equipment mounting positions, thus dispensing with stepladders of one sort or another. Attached to the undersides of the catwalks are horizontal masking planes, thus freeing up the overhead space from the usual teasers which make lighting so difficult. The catwalks also make it possible to feed spotlights via flexible cables directly from electronic dimmer packs located on the catwalks, thus eliminating permanently fixed branch circuits and plugging receptacles, and the natural tendency to leave spotlights hanging adjacent to them, a practice which accounts for more bad lighting in the theatre than any other single factor.

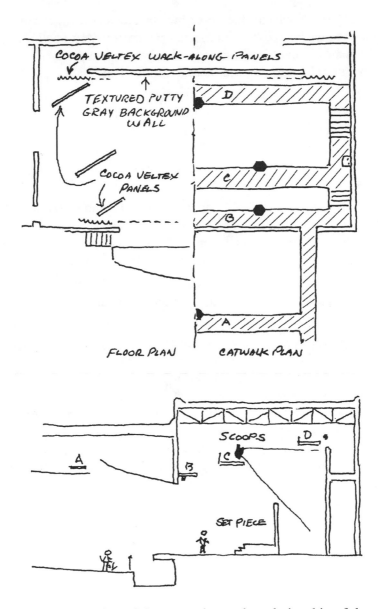

FLOOR PLAN   CATWALK PLAN

A cross-section of the stage shows the relationship of the cat-walks one to another in heights above the stage floor. The relationship of Catwalk C to D is of particular interest, for now, given properly sized and arranged freestanding scenery, it is possible to flood

114

the background wall by means of scoops mounted on Catwalk C. For a stage of this size three 14" scoops with 500-watt PS IF lamps for each color circuit will suffice. And the 40° maximum angle to the base of the background wall assures an exceptionally even color distribution.

If color can be distributed over the background wall in such an efficient manner, why not patterns as well? The section below shows the addition of a light source on the downstage side of Catwalk C. Thus the shadow of any silhouette placed at the upstage side of this catwalk will fall upon the background wall, and the clarity of the shadow will depend upon the compactness of the light source, plus, of course, the distance of this light source from the silhouette, which in this case is a practical maximum of 48". An elevation of this new arrangement is shown below.

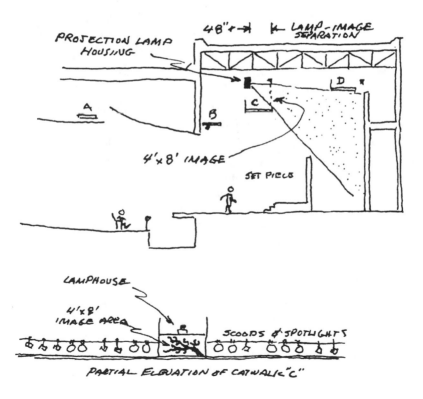

In the elevation above a large tree limb, with leaves, will make a good starter for experimentation. Light from the projection lamp in the lamphouse provides the silhouette and the sky coloring while the scoops turned on at a low intensity can touch up the shadow area. For a sunset scene, try an orange color filter near the projection lamp and chocolate color filters in a trio of scoops.

Using the foliage projection, with an orange gel at the lamphouse aperture and chocolate gels in a circuit of scoops, we would have an orange sky at dusk with velvety brown leaf shadows. Substitute a medium blue gel at the lamphouse and yellow green gels in the scoops and we have the effect of a jungle by day. With the cardboard cutout in the design of a stained glass window, colored gels can be taped over the cutouts and the scoops gelled in deep violet and we have the effect of a dimly lit cathedral nave. The possibilities are endless.

With all this, the astonishing fact is that the colors do not seem to blend or wash each other out. Rather, they seem to retain their true visual identity, at least to the mind's eye. What we are experiencing is an example of the "persistence of vision."

Image materials range from natural objects such as the above, all the way to artifacts such as stage lighting color media fitted together, overlapped, or used to cover profiled holes in opaque materials. These are in addition to the more traditional painting with transparent dyes on transparent media, including the clear acetate sheets Wilfred used. The shape and size of a particular image depends, of course, on the dimensions of the background wall. The 4' x 8' image area noted above is just an average size from past experience. The image will usually be about one-fourth as large as the wall or other projection surface.

From the brief description of image materials it is obvious that we are approaching the more abstract art of "assemblages" or "collages." And the success of this background projection system depends in great part on a thorough understanding of the ambience of the stage space with which are are dealing. A visit to a modern art gallery will be useful. First study the pictures. Note that the more illusory the pictures are the more elaborately they are framed. The more abstract pictures have very simple frames, or none at all. Note also that sculptural pieces are displayed in pure space, away from walls. Similarly, scenery in space staging is akin to sculpture. This does not mean that literal detail is banished, but what there is of it must be in space, certainly not framed. From this it follows that any details projected upon the wall must likewise be on the abstract side, and should enlarge upon the scenic idea but definitely not expand the scenery itself.

Pale Yellow 07 field with Straw 12 taped over window openings

To demonstrate the flexibility of staging in such a theatre, one final example is given. First note on the stage floor plan the front traveler curtain of scrim and the rear curtain panels of a lightweight velour. Close the scrim curtain. Place the Oriental pavilion off center toward stage left. Arrange the rear curtain panels as shown in the sketch, with a portion of the background wall exposed, in proportion to a large Chinese scroll. Render the scrim opaque by the fill light. Then bring up the projection. Dim the fill a bit, then part the scrim and cross-fade from the projection to the actual pavilion. The cross-fade should include the scoops from Moss Green 89 to Sky Blue 68.

Limitations

Fifty years' experience in the theatre tells me that this particular projection system is best left in the boondocks for the fantastic enjoyment of those willing to follow the rules of "space staging." It is not a system for everyone. I am a living witness to this truth. My first work in this field had to do with remodelings and they were all successful. Later on I used these same ideas in new theatre construction and life became more difficult for me. In addition to architects and engineers, there were owners and the endless cycle of revolving door staff changes. It's one thing to bolt some 2 x 4s to a structure and hang a catwalk and quite another to forestall workmen busily running ducts and conduit across free spaces.

During the 1950s and 1960s I inserted the system into over a hundred new theatres, mostly multipurpose spaces for forum, concert and dramatic performance, spaces where a fly-loft was out of the question from the beginning of the planning, and the system did work rather well for those who took the trouble to understand the nature of the spaces and the artistic esthetics involved. And it is to these esthetics that we now turn.

Some Esthetics of Space Staging

It is obvious that if the projection is to come down over the scenery, the scenery will have to be truly freestanding. This is what makes it a "set piece." It is no longer a "picture" framed by the proscenium but it is, in effect, a piece of sculpture in space. A piece of sculpture in an art gallery is inherently more abstract than a picture in a frame. Naturally, a set piece for a play will contain many realistic details. But the fact that it is in space means that it will have a profile — a silhouette. The profile is most important — were all the details within the set piece removed the profile should still have significance. This is the key to designing scenery for space staging — the importance of profile. Here is the place where the realistic and the abstract merge.

The projection expands the environment of the set piece, but it must do so in a most suggestive manner. The one thing that it must not do is be a continuation of the realistic detail at the core of the set piece. For the same reason, foreground must never be taken into a projected scene. If sheep are grazing on a distant hill, let them graze on that distant hill. Do not run a nearby field up to the distant hill. In the example on the previous page, a partial projection isolates a pavilion on the mountain from the actual working set piece.

Mazda in Nirvana

That which I have already written I intended to be an overview of stage lighting, hitting the high points in an effort to be quick about it. Besides, you never know how lighting will turn out — in a way it is a very personal matter, a mercurial sort of magic.

Because of this a lighting man is a cynical dreamer. But he dreams on — so I decided to close this discussion with a dream of my own, the perfect dream of everything I want around me. In effect, the god Mazda in Nirvana.

The plan I would choose would be that of the proscenium, not because I like realistic scenery — I don't — but because entrances and exits are easily handled and lighting has a sense of direction. Staging would be in the form of store window display — mounds of scenery mainly castered: mounds so that the lighting can strike from many angles, castered so that the scenery doesn't have to ascend to the heavens.

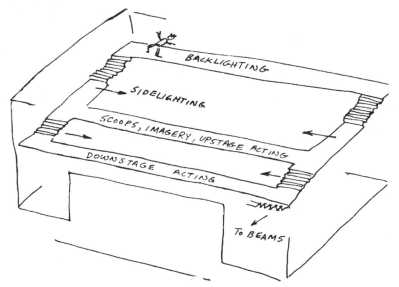

119

As to the heavens, they would be mine: the multiplaned catwalk system previously described upon which I could walk to mount, connect, adjust and, on occasion, operate the lights. Attached to the undersides of the walks would be a horizontal masking system.

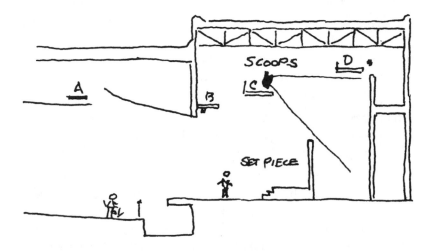

Of special interest is the freestanding background wall. Study carefully the relationship of Catwalks C and D and the background wall. By terminating the wall in space both the flooding of the wall and the imagery projected upon it from Catwalk C can be carried all the way to the top.

In addition to scenery projection, the catwalk system described on the preceding pages can be used to light freestanding scenery in display window style. On page 121 is shown the first lighting exercise with the catwalk mounting positions indicated.

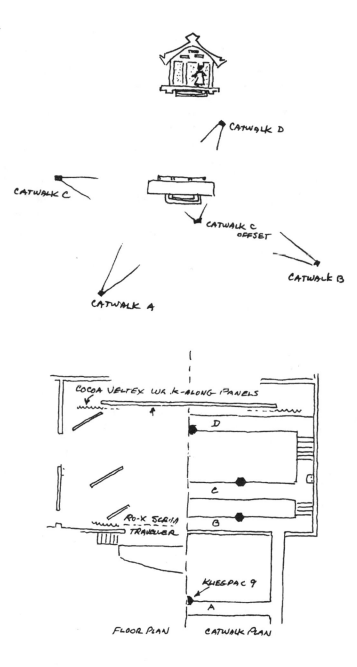

CATWALK D

CATWALK C

CATWALK C OFFSET

CATWALK B

CATWALK A

COCOA VELTEX WALK-ALONG PANELS

D

C

B

RO-X SCRIM TRAVELLER

KLIEGPAC 9

A

FLOOR PLAN   CATWALK PLAN

121

As in store window display, the lighting must be highly selective, yet essentially soft-edged where spill upon the surrounding neutral surfaces is unavoidable. In window display the R and PAR lamps have fields which are sufficiently ragged. On stage Fresnels or ellipsoidals with diffusions filters are more practical.

The freestanding background wall also serves as an entrance and exit baffle. Side masking is served by a series of framed panels rotating on pins set at the tops and bottoms of the offstage leading edges, much in the manner of luans. The panels are covered with Veltex cloth, a teasled velour from Valley Forge Fabrics, Ft. Lauderdale, Florida. Veltex looks like duveytine but is highly opaque and more durable. The walk-along traveler curtains to the rear and the undersides of the horizontal masking system are also of the same teasled velour.

The RO-X scrim traveler curtain is of a boucle weave and opaque or semitransparent, depending upon the nature of the lighting. It is excellent for fog and mist, dissolves, and visions. It is also acoustically transparent.

I show Kliegpac 9 portable electronic dimmer units on the catwalks. With this solution you eliminate a lot of wires and also a patch panel. Power is brought directly to the packs and the dimmers are controlled at a place of your choosing by low voltage controllers. The conventional solution is by circuitry which terminates at a centrally located patch panel. An advantage to this solution is more flexibility in selecting the type of dimmers, using both electronic and autotransformer. For some very subtle cues I still like the old dial-type autotransformer.

In Summary

I am assuming that by selecting this book your back was already to the wall and you are seeking every possible shortcut. Since there are many ways to an end I have not spent a great deal of time with specimen setups: they could be both encyclopedic and confusing. However, here are some points to keep in mind.

When you survey a site for stage lighting, check out the existing illumination and see if there is anything you can use, especially if it is dimmable or can be kept at a low level. This will mean that you can add highlighting instead of having to start from scratch. Remember that you can go a long way with the various PAR lamps, from homemade "stovepipe" units to commercial supply at a fraction of the cost of Fresnel and ellipsoidal spotlights...that is, if you don't need the variable beams or precision cutoffs. Of the Fresnels and ellipsoidals, the 6" and 8" are standards, but select those that use lamps that are easily replaced. And with electronic dimming, availability of service is essential.

The merchandising directories I listed at the beginning of the book are both detailed and complete. The following are the names and addresses of firms whose literature you would be likely to find on my office shelf:

Altman Stage Lighting Co. Inc.
57 Alexander St.
Yonkers, NY 10701
(good spotlights)

Superior Electric Co.
383 Middle St.
Bristol, CT 06010
(possible source for some reliable autotransformer dimmers)

Electronics Diversified, Inc.
1675 N.W. 216th Ave.
Hillsboro, OR 97124
(good portable dimmers)

Vara-Light/Dimatronics
6207 Commercial Rd.
Crystal Lake, IL 60014
(repairs old autotransformer dimmers)

Great American Market
826 North Cole Ave.
Hollywood, CA 90038
(good line of patterns and projection equipment)

Rosco Laboratories
36 Bush Ave.
Port Chester, NY 10573
(color media and translucent backdrops)

Olesen Co.
1535 Ivar Ave.
Hollywood, CA 90028
(good general catalog)

James Hull Miller, a graduate of Princeton, combines an academic background in literature and philosophy with many years of actual theatre experience of which twelve were spent in teaching. Since 1958 he has been a freelance designer and consultant. His field of special interest is the development of a new stagecraft for the theatre which takes the form of *freestanding scenery*. He has designed numerous open-stage theatres based on this system of stagecraft for colleges, communities, student unions, schools and churches. For many years he maintained a scenic studio, the **Arts Lab**, in Shreveport, Louisiana, where he gave workshops as well as constructed sets for use in a variety of spaces. A filmstrip on self-supporting scenery that was photographed in the lab is available from Contemporary Drama Service. Other titles currently available include **Self-Supporting Scenery** (the basic text), **Small Stage Sets on Tour**, and **Stagecraft for Christmas and Easter Plays.**

Miller is a Charter Member of the U.S. Institute for Theatre Technology and in 1978 was named a Fellow of the Institute. He is a Founding Member of the American Society of Theatre Consultants. Presently he lives in Charlottesville, Virginia, with his wife Mundy.

NOTES

NOTES

NOTES

ORDER FORM

MERIWETHER PUBLISHING LTD.
P.O. BOX 7710
COLORADO SPRINGS, CO 80933
TELEPHONE: (719) 594-4422

Please send me the following books:

_____ **Stage Lighting in the Boondocks #TT-B141** $10.95
by James Hull Miller
A simplified guide to stage lighting

_____ **Self-Supporting Scenery #TT-B105** $10.95
by James Hull Miller
A scenic workbook for the open stage

_____ **Stagecraft for Christmas and Easter Plays** $9.95
#TT-B170
by James Hull Miller
A simplified method of staging in the church

_____ **Small Stage Sets on Tour #TT-B102** $9.95
by James Hull Miller
A practical guide to portable stage sets

_____ **Stagecraft I #TT-B116** $14.95
by William H. Lord
A complete guide to backstage work

_____ **Elegantly Frugal Costumes #TT-B125** $10.95
by Shirley Dearing
A do-it-yourself costume maker's guide

_____ **The Theatre and You #TT-B115** $14.95
by Marsh Cassady
An introductory text on all aspects of theatre

These and other fine Meriwether Publishing books are available at your local bookstore or direct from the publisher. Use the handy order form on this page.

NAME: _____

ORGANIZATION NAME: _____

ADDRESS: _____

CITY:_____ STATE: _____ ZIP: _____

PHONE: _____
  ❑ **Check Enclosed**
  ❑ **Visa or MasterCard #** _____

Signature: _____ *Date:* *Expiration* _____
     (required for Visa/Mastercard orders)

COLORADO RESIDENTS: Please add 3% sales tax.
SHIPPING: Include $2.75 for the first book and 50¢ for each additional book ordered.

  ❑ *Please send me a copy of your complete catalog of books and plays.*

ORDER FORM

MERIWETHER PUBLISHING LTD.
P.O. BOX 7710
COLORADO SPRINGS, CO 80933
TELEPHONE: (719) 594-4422

Please send me the following books:

———— **Stage Lighting in the Boondocks #TT-B141** $10.95
by James Hull Miller
A simplified guide to stage lighting

———— **Self-Supporting Scenery #TT-B105** $10.95
by James Hull Miller
A scenic workbook for the open stage

———— **Stagecraft for Christmas and Easter Plays** $9.95
#TT-B170
by James Hull Miller
A simplified method of staging in the church

———— **Small Stage Sets on Tour #TT-B102** $9.95
by James Hull Miller
A practical guide to portable stage sets

———— **Stagecraft I #TT-B116** $14.95
by William H. Lord
A complete guide to backstage work

———— **Elegantly Frugal Costumes #TT-B125** $10.95
by Shirley Dearing
A do-it-yourself costume maker's guide

———— **The Theatre and You #TT-B115** $14.95
by Marsh Cassady
An introductory text on all aspects of theatre

**These and other fine Meriwether Publishing books are available at
your local bookstore or direct from the publisher. Use the handy
order form on this page.**

NAME: _____

ORGANIZATION NAME: _____

ADDRESS: _____

CITY:_____ STATE: _____ ZIP: _____

PHONE: _____
  ❑ **Check Enclosed**
  ❑ **Visa or MasterCard #** _____

Signature: _____ *Date:* *Expiration* _____
      (required for Visa/Mastercard orders)

COLORADO RESIDENTS: Please add 3% sales tax.
SHIPPING: Include $2.75 for the first book and 50¢ for each additional book ordered.

  ❑ *Please send me a copy of your complete catalog of books and plays.*